One of Hilaire Belloc's friends to whom he lent the boat ('the boat' was the *Jersey* built in Jersey in 1845, employed as a pilot cutter and venerable even in 1931, 'the hulk' Hilaire Belloc called her) was Alan Phipps, Lieutenant RN, son of Sir Eric Phipps, the Ambassador who was plenipotentiary in Vienna at the time. Alan was an officer in destroyers in the mid 1930s. His destroyer was sunk in a naval battle in Greek waters in 1942, and he was killed soon after in commando action on the island of Leros. He was a charming, gay and vigorous young man, with a cork-like buoyancy on life's troubled seas.

Although a professional sailor, he confessed that navigation was not his forte and thought it a great joke that on a night passage in the *Jersey* he found he had for some time been sailing up the north coast of France, thinking he was sailing down the south coast of England. **

Of course, nobody would do anything so hare-brained as that nowadays.

Or would they?

---

*   *From Sailing with Mr Belloc.* Dermod MacCarthy. Collins Harvill. 1986

For Luis

Life's companion and gallant crew

SAILING WITH THE
ADMIRAL

by

MARTIN O'SCANNALL

Lodestar Books

Published 2019 by
Lodestar Books
71 Boveney Road, London, SE23 3NL, United Kingdom

lodestarbooks.com

Copyright © Martin O'Scannall 2019

All rights reserved.

A CIP catalogue record for this book
is available from the British Library

ISBN 978-1-907206-46-7

Typeset by Lodestar Books in Equity

Printed in the UK by Gomer Press Ltd

All papers used by Lodestar Books
are sourced responsibly

Contents

1	The Dilemma	7
2	The Ría del Eo	11
3	Killing the Demons	15
4	Weather-bound in Viveiro	19
5	One Hand in God's Pocket	25
6	Boatbuilding, Galician Fashion	30
7	Hello Darkness My Old Friend	33
8	Fires from a Pagan Past	36
9	At Close Quarters in Ferrol	40
10	Redes Regatta	47
11	Three Men in a Boat	51
12	Spring is Sprung	53
13	The Night Passage	58
	Interlude	62
14	On Mud Pies and Other Misadventures	64
15	Grumpy Old Men	67
16	'A Bit of a Chancer'	71
17	The Crystal City (and the perils of politics)	73
18	The Wreck of the 'Aegean Sea''	79
19	The Chiringuito in the Trees	83

20	The Great Mushroom Hunt	87
21	The Romance of a Proper Dinghy	89
22	La Costa de la Muerte	92
23	No Engine?	99
24	Blind Man's Buff	104
25	The Bar at Santa Marta de Ortigueira	108
26	Don Vicente Tofiño de San Miguel and Los Aguillones	115
27	The Winter List	120
28	The Stranding of the Howe and Other High Victorian Tales	124
29	In Sheltered Waters	135
30	A Cautionary Tale (Madness at Sea)	139
	Bibliography	141

1

The Dilemma

Imagine, for a moment, a bucolic scene.
   Old salt at the helm. Acolyte at his side. So many years, he is thinking. So many places. So many incidents. Dreaming in the heat of the afternoon. Not much happening. Drifting really. Tired. Yes, he is tired. A long night passage. Stars and all that. His thoughts turn to his ship. For it is *his* ship, an extension, almost of his being. For she is that familiar. *That* old. *That* strong. Yes of course. She talks, and he listens. She talks through what? The tiller for one, for it speaks. Of balance and things like that. The song, or whisper, or the moan of the wind. Of the murmur, or chuckle, or angry blow of a wave. Of a thousand things. For she and he are one.

Think Yehudi Menuhin and that violin. That kind of thing.

Where are we this time?

Somewhere where, if truth be told, he would rather not be. For his memories are of a gentler place, the creeks and inlets of the East Coast. That magical world, harsh of climate, but a balm to the soul, wild, desolate, flat, oh so flat, tidal, everything was tidal, and mud, always mud. And the birds. A kind of imagined homeland now. For exile, voluntary or not, is a bit like that.

But here. Well yes, it is spectacular. Awesome almost. A place of superlatives. Wild. Beautiful. Dangerous. The *rías altas* of North West Spain. Celtic. Stormy. Mysterious. Tiptoe here. For this is truly a desperate coast. Though sometimes...

'Topsail skipper?'

'No.'

Should have done of course. Getting old. This infernal heat. And no wind.

'How many have you caught Luis?'

'Seven.'

'Gosh!'

We drift on. Over the bow somewhere in this treacherous gulf is our destination, Ribadeo. A river. Rocks. Reefs. Nasty tides. Leading marks. Concrete piles. Ruddy great road bridge. Mucks up the ría no end does that. No space. But Caroline lives there. And we love Caroline. Enough to make this passage to surprise her. And then party. 'Treacherous gulf', for it is. It is called the Golfo de Foz, and, ask a local, it is feared. As much almost as the headlands we have passed, Cabo Ortegal, Estaca de Bares, are feared, woven into memory, dreaded and formidable. And somehow loved. Nay revered. This is Celtic territory after all. Every rock, every reef, every shoal a name. And a legend. And a saint. Or a pagan god. Or both. Yes, both for sure. Canny these Celts. Like, I would guess South West Ireland, or Scotland, or maybe Brittany. In fact, exactly like South West Ireland, for my ship and I have been there. Mizen Head in an Atlantic storm.

From ashore that one.

And the people, but we will come to the people.

Something modern and delicate passes in our lee. A kind of butterfly. Bound west. Us east. Modern, we are not modern. The opposite in fact. Obstinately old fashioned, curmudgeonly if you will. The ship. Launched in 1913. Yacht of the time. Elegant. All sheer. Grace. Beauty. Which you, in your devotion, work to enhance. You revel in that. The craftsmen. The times. The memories. And the skipper. Three score years and ten. And all that jazz.

For it is hard to take life too seriously, until that is…

(God how I distrust accounts of storms at sea).

We are hit by, ahem, the most violent wind it has ever been my pleasure to encounter.

Most upsetting.

In fact, pardon my French, *bloody terrifying*.

This thing has got it in for us. No mistake. Embayed. We can just, but only just, carry the foresail, (and nothing else) which being that of a gaff cutter is of a sensible size. On this awful coast. Oh, for the Stour, or the Orwell, or the Deben. But we had better, I suppose deal with this.

You know all too well the alternatives. Run for it and risk being overwhelmed in the entrance. Or attempt, lee shore under your lee, (rather obviously for where else would a ******** lee shore be?), the eighty nautical miles to Gijon. Ugh. How about *salvamento marítimo?* says Caroline over the airwaves. Ooh that sounds nice. Really comforting. Seductively so. Yes Caroline, you say, idiotically. For it is in fact. No. Don't be silly. Cowardly.

So to hell with it. We run on in. And we get away with it. *Much too exciting*, reads the log. Surfed we did in the entrance. Waves breaking all over the shop. Defied the odds, yet again. For we had met, all unsuspecting, something which the Admiralty pilot describes, in that lovely deadpan prose, thus:

Galernas. 1.154. General Information. The Galerna is a sudden, violent, NW wind that typically affects the coastal zone from Santander to Capbreton. Galernas usually appear between June and September, with the greatest frequency between July and August, mostly in the afternoon between 1400 and 1700 local time. They are particularly dangerous because of their extreme severity and sudden onset. Typical Galernas develop when the morning wind is initially either calm or light south. In hot conditions, temperatures quickly increase to around 27º to 30º C before midday and continue to rise in the early afternoon. A Galerna begins to be likely as soon as there is an 8º difference between the air temperature and the sea surface temperature. During the Galerna, air temperature drops rapidly, often by 12º and usually to the sea surface temperature. The wind suddenly veers NW and increases to force 8 or 9.

Biscay Pilot NP22

See. Useful the pilot. Incomparable in fact.

Ask ashore and you will get this, or something like it:

> Hay una palabra sería, con regusto de sal y de lágrimas, un galicismo hondo y temible, sonoro y lúgubre, que va siempre enlazado al holocausto de las gentes pescadoras del Cantábrico: la galerna.
>
> Rafael González Echegaray.

Which is a poet's way of saying that it is a widow maker.*

More prosaically it is called, by the meteorologists, a Coastally Trapped Disturbance, the subject of learned and rather impenetrable papers, the gist of which is take a mountainous coast, extreme heat and temperature inversion in the upper atmosphere, and what you may or may not get, for it is impossible to forecast, is a rip roaring cold front, duration hours or days. It all depends. Equally prosaically, in electing to run in rather than run down the coast, there was more than an element of 'surely a wind of this strength cannot last.' And nor did it.

But one never knows.

All in all, rather sobering.

---

* *Sabado de la Gloría.* 20th April 1878. Over 300 fishermen lost their lives in that storm.

2

The Ría del Eo

You enter a different world. Earth not water. Trees not rocks. Fields, not waves. Even the smell…

That West Country feel. Complete with Friesians.

The wind has gone.

We are a companionable lot around the table, Caroline and husband Rufo, Pete with Carlos and Marina, his crew, Juan, the neighbour with his guitar. Luis is doing his barbecue act. Those seven fish he caught on passage. We are in the garden, twilight turns to starlit night. Fairy lights under the pine trees, reminiscence in the air. Down in the marina the talk had all been of that wind, the more improbable the estimate, the taller the story. But that is behind us now. Peter chuckles.

'Caroline just nabbed me, put me on the helm of *Eltoraji* and told me to get Martin and tow him in.'

Which is true. Into the *ría* we had shot, still with that banshee wind, Luis preparing the anchor, for there is room to do that, when to my astonishment that little blue gaffer, *Eltoraji* (we will meet her later) appeared, a tow was passed, and we were tucked up in the marina alongside Pete's aristocratic Morgan Giles *Martlet*, the very same incidentally that appears in that forbidding tome, *Heavy Weather Sailing*, by Adlard Coles.

Pete starts on the squeezebox. Juan begins to croon, Juan the writer, Juan the gentleman personified, Juan the old friend of Caroline. Friends around a table. What more can you ask? Wine flows all too freely, the fish arrives with a flourish.

Oops. Too long in the bucket. That heat. No ice.

Never mind.

Music ruled. As did those stars.

Tomorrow we will visit *Los Pachos* again. Pepe, the retired wooden boatbuilder, and his wife. Wind up a country lane or two, high above the ría, and here you will find their bar, quite alone surrounded by fields. A backwater and a bar *de toda la vida*, that Galician expression, albeit we are in Asturias, which means unchanged, from generation to generation, for here you may buy a few groceries, the odd vegetable, a packet of detergent, a box of matches, sit and play cards, noisily, for hour after hour, a kind of community centre, where the local bobby, Suso, a *policía local*, meaning the gentler side of the law, pops in for a gossip, for there is little for him to do. His beat is Castropol and Figueras; Castropol shuttered, elegant and aloof, that oddly Italianate hilltop village, crowned by church spire, the preserve of the aristocrat fallen on hard times, deserted streets, no shops, no bars, for such as there are lie far below, on the waterfront, perhaps the occasional drunk, *move along now*, but not much else. You wait.

The invitation comes.

Up the stairs. Door unlocked. Pepe's museum.

A little hidden jewel. Scores of ship models. All shapes and sizes. Sometimes in a quiet moment you will catch him down in the bar, making the next one. Painstaking work, for he does not count the hours that go into the making of a ship model, faithful to the last detail. A sailing ship? A square-rigger? A Thames barge? His wife stitches the sails. A coaster, a paddle steamer, a skiff. How do you manage the stanchions, the anchor, the navigation lights? The retired master boatbuilder, building boats still, but in miniature. Door carefully closed again, we lean on the rail, overlooking the ría. Which is more in the way of an estuary. Encumbered by shoals. Woodland opposite. Drying inlets. The bones of the old ships. And gossip, as one does, of boats, of tides, of the weather, and the ways of a world gone mad.

Until next time.

Later, across the *ría*, in Ribadeo, we will pay a visit to Claudio, the harbourmaster, by custom a retired Master in the Merchant Marine, who despite the formality of his position, indeed his powers, which are considerable, is affability personified. A long meandering gossip, a fossicking through the old ship registers, for time was when trade hereabouts came all by sea, the roads being what they were, and bless me, he too makes ship models, but this time to commission, for the Ría del Eo is home to *Astilleros Gondán*, and they build ships for North Sea work, for Norway mostly, and at launch time, the shipowner is presented with a model of the newly launched vessel—*one thousand seven hundred hours, this one will take*—for it is his little side-line, when not sitting in that tower, overlooking the mouth of the *ría*, presiding over all things nautical. For coasters come still. That tricky dogleg, under the road bridge, the horse in the middle of the *ría* to be avoided and a tiny pilot boat to help. Fussily shepherding the ship. For so narrow is the navigable channel, she must enter, and then turn in her own length, before backing down to the timber quay. Eucalyptus, the bane of Galicia, and a commercial crop *par excellence*.

And down in the *ría* are the *botes del Eo*, the ones Pepe used to build, and the ones that the next generation, Martin, still makes, the last wooden boat-builders on the Eo. The *ría* half dead now, the tide mills in ruins, the skills lost, the rotten bones of once fine ships. But Martin hangs on, just, always the same craft, of wood, open, the design unchanged for as long as anybody can remember, for these were the fishing craft, sail and oar—a precarious way to earn a living at the best of times—but now built for folk who like to sail for pleasure. And a fine spectacle they make, with their near lateen sail, mainsheet in one hand, tiller in the other, heeling to the breeze in the *ría*, (the smaller the boat, the greater the pleasure), and at rest, side by side, in the marina, for a place is especially set aside for the *botes del Eo*, a sight for sore eyes. Grace and purpose amongst gracelessness. Down to the creek, under a bridge, past the saltings, sheep grazing, is a shed, a ramp, a trolley and in the shed the latest *bote del Eo*, Martin working on. A lonely life, for he has no apprentice. Are we interrupting? No? But even if we were, politeness wins the day.

A wooden boatyard is a wooden boatyard the world over. Shavings, cobwebs, dust, spars in the rafters, wood piles outside, seasoning, the giant bandsaw, the workbench, and on trestles, the next *bote del Eo*. The moulds stacked in a corner now, for she is well advanced. A good sheer. An almost wineglass transom stern. A powerful flared bow. A heavy craft as befits her former trade, fishing. Embellished now with iroko gratings, she will join the others out in the ría, the fleet of *los Pachos*, the last wooden boatbuilders on the Eo.

Tucked away as such places tend to be, at the head of a tidal creek, away from anywhere much, you wonder if you could get your ship up here. But no. It is too silted up now. Later, you will find just such a place, but that is later.

Hungry?

You are spoiled for choice. But the best bet is where the workers from *Astilleros Gondán* eat in their lunch-break. The shipyard siren blows. They pour out, like those black and white films of old, Titanic style. *That* is where you eat. Munch, quaff, enjoy, *que aproveche,* that companionable Spanish hail fellow, well met, 'do enjoy your meal', greeting.

Coffee, brandy, cigarette.

Siren goes again.

And they are gone.

As must we.

3

Killing the Demons

The demons being, of course, your own.

You survey the Golfo de Foz with renewed distaste. The weather with sceptical eye. Wind north now, but it will back, just you wait. It will back. August. That treacherous month. Between two gales. The smudge on the horizon. That is Punta Roncadoiro, the one you must clear.

Pete tows you out. You could of course have sailed it. But we are in company. What takes him ten minutes would take you two hours, beating back and forth in the entrance, against the seas and the tide, rock spits to port, rock spits to starboard, a nasty old place in all conscience, for you are never all that comfortable in such confined, confused and sloppy waters.

Like a bad-tempered bath.

Clear at last, and despite little wind, you have a reef in. For you trust this gulf not at all. And perhaps with justification.

> Squalls, descending from the mountains and funnelled by the valleys are experienced in the Golfo de Foz and up to 12 miles offshore when the wind farther offshore is E to WSW. They are especially violent off the ría de Foz and the coast NW to Burela.
>
> *Biscay Pilot NP22*

There it is again, 'especially violent.' (Well just wait until you meet HMS *Bossington*).

We tiptoe slowly onwards.

And sure enough the wind backs. You can no longer lay the course. We stand in towards Puerto de Alúmina, curious for a closer look. It looks no more appealing than it did last time. Worse in fact, for there are off-lying islets, a buoy serving no obvious purpose and clouds of dust. Weather eye, as always open. And partly on the clouds. For they will tell of wind. How so? Because you remember another occasion, in this very same gulf, Ribadeo bound. Behind the coastal plain are mountains, and above the peaks, clouds. Fluffy white variety. All innocent. One moment stationary. The next moving and moving fast. Hum. Something happening up there. A lot of wind. And sure enough, no sooner in and safe and sound, it comes. That sudden blast.

No *galerna* today. No chance of that. But happy you are not. We plug on, stand off again, stand in again, Pete vanished over the horizon, and slowly, infinitely slowly, Punta Roncadoiro looms larger. The day wears on. The wind is taking off now. You pay the price for your timidity. You will be lucky to make Viveiro before the light goes.

But you do at last clear the point. Ease the sheets. Relax.

A wide *ría*, clear of dangers, wooded hills, and way up ahead that enormous breakwater, for they build them big here and with good reason. Behind the breakwater the fishing fleet lies. And beyond that again, mercifully out of bounds for one with no engine, a marina. Reached up a long and dreary cut. View, a supermarket and a good deal of traffic. A marine version of a car park and about as exciting.

But we have what? Eight miles to go. And no real wind. But still waters. You are happy. The Golfo de Foz is behind you. You have not been here before.

Feel way in to anchor at midnight, reads the log entry.

Which was balm to the soul.

Yes, exactly that. Gone was the tediousness and restlessness of the marina in Ribadeo. Instead, here we are, in no hurry, in a lovely tree girt *ría*, wind fading, light fading, but slipping along in that way *Sauntress* has, that odd ability to sail in no apparent wind, a new place hidden in the darkness, to reveal itself at dawn, swinging the lead now, 7 fathoms, 6 fathoms, 5 fathoms, mud. Oh yes, mud. For arm the lead and then you know.

'That will do Luis. Let go the anchor.'

Set the anchor light, that dioptric lens in the foretriangle, which is where it should be, not some pinpoint masquerading as a star atop a soaring masthead.

Big drink and to bed.

Where you dream, so to speak, of days past.

And characters. No lack of these here, for amongst the dreary conformity of modern yachtsmen in modern marinas with their oh so frightfully modern, oh so frightfully expensive yachts, bristling with technology and vulgar ostentation… And what, I ask, happened to affordability? For after the war and up until the advent of GRP, the ordinary mortal could get afloat quite modestly in decent craft, built in wood, some to a set design, and armed with charts, compass, lead line or echo sounder, maybe later an RDF set, get around in reasonable safety and, more to the point have *fun* in the process, all without breaking the bank. Among the dreary conformity, as I was saying, two characters stood out, Mr Enigma and Mad Marc.

Mr Enigma stood out, well no, in fact the opposite, for he was a retiring kind of person, by reason first of his boat, which though old, Dutch, and steel, a heavy craft to wit, was impeccable and which he handled beautifully. And second because in some curious way, things did not add up. It was not just that he was the epitome of the bemused Englishman abroad, not quite chewing the top of his umbrella, though that seemed strange after ten years at sea. It was the oddity of his domestic arrangements, into which we will not delve, but somehow seemed tinged with menace, allied with the vagueness of his intentions, (again none of our business), but above all, I think, the thought that here is a man with a touch of the Jeeves (all that brain power) floating aimlessly around in a cloud of mystery.

A spy, we decided in that schoolboy way.

Mad Marc, by contrast, would never be found chewing the top of his umbrella, even supposing he had one, which I doubt. What he did have, however, was a travel stained yacht, with a broken engine, a teddy bear in the rigging and a crew for which the word rowdy could have been invented. A true *matelot*, of *Les Filles d'Amsterdam* variety. And the night before we were supposed to depart to do battle with the Golfo de Foz, when we should be resting (fat chance), this trio turned up royally drunk (a magnetic force so far as Luis is concerned, for if Luis has a weakness, it is…), so we were perforce swept into the party. A circumnavigator, as he proved by producing a petrol drum sized container of Malgache rum, in return for Galician *aguardiente*, which we just happened to have aboard, he announced that his life's ambition, having completed his circumnavigation, was to fuck an ostrich.

And whose advances still drunk, on Caroline in the morning, *unhand me varlet*, were a wonder to behold.

Never a dull moment, cruising.

Particularly perhaps if in need of a meal ashore. Where, hungry you go, naturally enough to a place called, *Sailor's Bar*, (as in *Hello Sailor?*).

To be greeted by this:

MENU

Octopus to the party (pulpo a feira)

Courageous potatoes (patatas bravas)

Huge hairspray with grelos (lacón con grelos)

Female Jews with thief (judias con chorizo)

Pretty to the iron (bonito a la plancha)

Oh, and

Wines from the river (Ribeiro)

Better read aloud. Gerard Hoffnung, that master of timing, would have done it justice. And more. But who, I wonder, remembers him now?

4

Weather-bound in Viveiro

Fate and the War Office chose that I should spend three years living and working in Baghdad. Sent for two years I happily stayed on for a third, but rejected, wisely as it turned out, the invitation to serve a fourth. This was an unusual military appointment in as much I was granted a commission in the Iraqi Army by a special Royal 'Irada,' wore Iraqi uniform and was paid direct by the Iraqi Government.

These years were 1950/54. Prince Abdul was Regent for his young nephew, the boy King Feisal II. Nur-es-Said was the Prime Minister and most of the senior ministerial appointments by equally veteran and ageing men who had arrived with King Feisal I from the Hejaz to run the newly created kingdom after the First World War.

Boy King, Regent and Prime Minister were all to be assassinated not long after my departure. I personally knew all the Regicides. I am far from certain, had I still been there, that my departure would have been peaceful.

K. J. Whitehead. Iraq The Irremediable. Harwich 1989
Martin, from Kenneth, August 1989

We are almost, you might think in Lawrence of Arabia land, and you would not be altogether wrong. But you need to shift the focus a little, think Blondie Hasler, Mike Richie, *Jester* and the Hasler vane gear. And that rather acid comment about affordable sailing. Because that is where

Kenneth fits it. His boat was a French designed reverse sheer double-ended strip planked Bermudian sloop of a class named *Grand Diable*, called *Clairon*. Length overall 30 feet. Kept rather improbably in Newhaven, alongside *Jester* (Kenneth was a contemporary of both Blondie Hasler and Mike Richie and knew both) and fitted with the Hasler vane gear, nicknamed *Esmeralda*.

Kenneth, as befitted a man of his generation and background, had his club, The Savile Club in Brook Street, his favourite cigarette *Abdulla*, a monocle, a deep knowledge of the classical world (*Iraq the Irremediable* was a model of erudition) and an utter contempt for the material, especially motor cars.

He was also completely fearless.

And when I write of the *mistral*, or the *bora*, or the *meltemi*, it is because I was aboard *Clairon*, with Kenneth, to learn of such things and a better mentor in the art of cruising you could not wish to meet. For twenty or so years he cruised the Mediterranean aboard *Clairon*, and for summer after summer I used to join him. Salt stained ensign of the Royal Ocean Racing Club and all. Frugal would be an understatement. And marketing with Kenneth was a revelation. He had very strong views on what was and what was not worth buying, a particular contempt, I remember, for so-called peaches, *not worth eating my boy*. And nor would it be worth going back to those places now. They are changed beyond recognition, but in those days, primitive, solitary (virtually no other yachts) and very, very foreign.

And his was the remark, if things became difficult at sea, *un peu de courage* and his bible, *The Admiralty Pilot*. Admiralty charts, insurance at Lloyds and, by telegram, *At X expect you on… bring 200 Abdulla*.

Oh yes. I nearly forgot, the ceremony of the new moon.

And somehow, the love of the Admiral has stuck. He is thorough, accurate and to the point. Of waypoints there are none, thank God. Of marinas nothing. Of restaurants, attractions, local colour, none. But as a pilot, *sans pareil*. A constant companion on this wild and seductive coast. And the Spanish equivalent *Derrotero de la Costa NW de España La Estaca de Bares al Rio Miño*, equally rigorous.

And I will find my own restaurant, thank you very much.

Next morning Pete attempted to leave, in not awfully promising weather.

Some hours later he was back, reporting squalls. Consult the Admiral and sure enough:

Cabo Estaca de Bares (…) Hazards. Local intensification of winds has been reported. In February 1966 HMS *Bossington* (425 tonnes) seeking shelter from a SW gale force 9 encountered winds of F11 to 12 in Ría del Barqueiro. During SW and W gales, squalls blow down from Piedras Canoles 43°45′N, 7°42′W.

The locals would simply say *muy jodido*. Don't mess.

Superfluous, perhaps to say, that the *Admiralty Pilot* is meant to be read with the Admiralty chart, in this case, my passage planning chart 1290 Cabo de San Lorenzo to Cabo Ortegal, and a quick check locates Piedras Canoles 43°45′N, 7°42′W, pretty much where Pete called it a day.

And no shame in that.

'No Luis, I do not believe Kenneth was a spy. But he over-wintered on this coast somewhere. I remember him saying that it was a protestant community and that he wrote letters for them. Would you know where that might be?'

'That would probably have been Muros, in the *rías baixas*.'

It would also have been in Franco's time, late 1960s early 1970s I would judge. When Spain was a very closed place, excepting perhaps the first beginnings of the *Costa del Sol* and all that. But not here.

The old photographs, not to mention Luis' reminiscences, speak of a very simple life indeed. So the story makes sense. Literacy would be far from universal. And it is a typical Kenneth gesture. Give not take. And he did it in another way. Yes, he relied on the *Admiralty Pilot*, but he also compiled comprehensive cruising notes for those who might follow, recognised by the award, more than once, of the Cruising Association Brittan Cup. One sits by me as I write. *1984. Major J Whitehead*. Pewter, a bit battered.

And for reading the detail on the Admiralty chart his little brass tortoise, with a magnifying glass in his back, still used for exactly that. So you see, *Sauntress* carries memories.

Many memories.

'What do you think Pete?'

'Don't like it. The French are giving gales.'

Enough said. We wait.

And mull over a small puzzle. That Protestant community. In severely Catholic Spain, or more properly Galicia, home to Santiago de Compostela, the Inquisition and those hated *diezmos* (the tithe which said ten percent of your crops, your livestock, the produce of your land, goes to the Church). But this facile generalisation masks something much more interesting. For dig around a bit. And what do you find?

This for one:

THE BIBLE IN SPAIN

or

The Journeys, Adventures, and Imprisonments
of an Englishman, in an Attempt to
circulate the Scriptures in the Peninsula

by

GEORGE BORROW

Date of publication 1842. Which is what? More than a century and a half ago. No matter. Say *Don Jorgito el Inglés* to Luis, or indeed any Galician and they will know, immediately, to whom you are referring. Such is memory. The book was a resounding success, a rollicking ride through a country torn by the Carlist Wars, *posadas*, bandits, filth, mules, guides, clutching his supply of 'the Scriptures' foisted on all and sundry, the local notary for one, and you have, as the title says, a number one, gold plated, Boy's Own adventure story. No wonder they lapped it up.

And *Don Jorgito el Inglés*, in his five years of travels for the Bible Society in the Peninsula, did not forget Galicia. Heaven forbid. But he had a hard time of it. *Blessed with a magnificent physique, and an unswerving belief in God's beneficence; endowed with 'the gift of tongues' and a cheerful disposition, George Borrow was well equipped for life.* So says the Editor's note. And just as well. He reaches Finisterre. Is arrested by the *alcalde* on suspicion of being the Carlist pretender, (*but I am English* cutting no ice), and is about to be shot along with his luckless guide when:

> 'The safest plan after all,' said the *alcalde*, 'appears to be, to send you both prisoners to Corcuvion, where the head alcalde can dispose of you as he thinks proper. You must, however, pay for your escort; for it is not to be supposed that the housekeepers of Finisterra have nothing else to do than to ramble about the country with every chance fellow who finds his way to this town.'
>
> 'As for that matter,' said Antonio, 'I will take charge of them both. I am the *valiente* of Finisterra, and fear no two men living. Moreover, I am sure that the captain here will make it worth my while, else he is no Englishman. Therefore, let us be quick and set out for Corcuvion at once, as it is getting late. First of all, however, captain, I must search you and your baggage. You have no arms, of course? But it is best to make all sure.'
>
> Long ere it was dark I found myself again on the pony, in company with my guide, wending our way along the beach in the direction of Corcuvion. Antonio de la Trava tramped heavily on before, his musket on his shoulder.
>
> Myself. —Are you not afraid, Antonio, to be thus alone with two prisoners, one of whom is on horseback? If we were to try, I think we could overpower you.
>
> Antonio de la Trava. —I am the *valiente de Finisterra*, and I fear no odds.
>
> Myself. —Why do you call yourself the *valiente* of Finisterra?
>
> Antonio de la Trava. —The whole district call me so. When the French came to Finisterra, and demolished the fort, three perished by my hand. I stood on the mountain, up where I saw you scrambling to-day. I continued firing at the enemy, until three detached themselves in pursuit of me. The fools! Two perished amongst the rocks by the fire of this musket, and as for the third, I beat his head to pieces with the stock. It is on that account that

they call me the *valiente* of Finisterra.

    Myself. —How came you to serve with the English fleet? I think I heard you say that you were present when Nelson fell.

    Antonio de la Trava. —I was captured by your countrymen, captain; and as I had been a sailor from my childhood, they were glad of my services. I was nine months with them, and assisted at Trafalgar. I saw the English admiral die. You have something of his face, and your voice, when you spoke, sounded in my ears like his own. I love the English, and on that account, I saved you.

Skin of his teeth. Such a strange little cameo of the death of Lord Nelson. But what George Borrow should have known, and indeed was sharply reminded, is that when you are called *El Valiente de Finisterra*, it is not a name you give yourself, it is a name you are given, just as he was given the name *Jorgito el Inglés*, or I *El Irlandés*, or, and we will meet him later, the hermit who was *O Alemán de Camelle*.

And as for Kenneth, materialising, so to speak, in whichever fishing community it was, Abdullah, monocle, crumpled tweeds and all, the epitome of the English Milord, he would most surely have been given *his* particular name.

And by that he will be remembered to this day.

The pity is we do not know where.

Now, since we are fossicking around in history, in a rather desultory kind of way, here is a little story. Aboard *Sauntress*, especially made for the ship, is a forged seam rake, a thing of beauty, for I watched its making, the water cascading, the bellows blasting, the anvil ringing, red hot iron twirling in deft and practiced hands. And when it was done, back straightened, hands wiped on leather apron, came this:

'You know we made fittings for the Spanish Armada.'

Said as though it was yesterday.

5

One Hand in God's Pocket

Morning brought a land breeze.

On the wings of which *Sauntress* slipped seaward. Eight miles to the entrance, leaving behind *Martlet*, for she, with engine, could follow later, and leaving behind too, memories of Viveiro, the busker, who seeing Pete, Luis and I seated at a table, remarked

'You look like pirates.'

A complement accepted as such.

And that thing, rare as hen's teeth nowadays, a watchmaker, grimy window, fob watches hanging, clock in pieces on the counter, a workshop so small and modest, it would be all too easy to miss. The proprietor in the evening of his years, glasses, for this trade is hard on the eyes. And when he is gone? Nothing. Romantic? Nostalgic even? To the observer, perhaps. But to Martin back in Ribadeo, building yet another *bote del Eo*, or the watchmaker, repairing yet another watch, nothing of the kind.

Work, just work.

The land breeze was failing. Which was to be expected. Morning breeze, a pause and then the true wind would fill in. That at least is the theory. I had put the ship equidistant between the two headlands which marked the entrance and this for a reason. A ship with no engine relies on the wind, which being so, you keep as far clear of the land as you can. Too many have been lost, not in storms, but becalmed, in the grip of some current, set helpless on the rocks. Simple really.

Bumpy. Still no wind.

Not a very nautical term, bumpy. But graphic. And the truth. Bumpy and infuriating. For there was the faintest breeze in which normally *Sauntress* would revel. But thrown this way and that she did not have a chance. Pete passed in our lee and was gone. The hours passed.

'We have a nice northeaster,' announced Pete over the airwaves.

'Well we do not,' was the huffy rejoinder.

What we did have was a spiffing view of Los Aguillones.

A propos, the Admiral has something to say. You close the *Biscay Pilot* NP22 and open the *West Coasts of Spain and Portugal Pilot* NP67, disgracefully old, you have to admit, but *rocks don't move do they* is the not very convincing excuse.

Anyway, here is the Admiral. Who after a lot of useful preliminary stuff on such things as *Maritime Topography, Currents, and Tidal Streams, Abnormal* (ouch!) *waves, Climates and weather, storms, fronts, winds, squalls* (we know all about those), and a good many etcetera's, gets down to business.

> Between Cabo Ortegal, which is described in the *Biscay Pilot*, and Punta Candelaria (8 miles WSW), the coast, rugged and precipitous, is backed by several well-defined summits and is indented by a small bay. To the W of the bay, the coastline, known as Fronton de Candelaria, is lofty, rugged and inaccessible with many rocky pinnacles sloping down to the sea and is dominated by Monte Candelaria.

In short, perfectly horrible.

But the language is almost poetic. *Lofty, rugged, precipitous, inaccessible, indented, rocky pinnacles*. But there is something else about the Admiral (whilst we go nowhere much slowly) which is this. They (the Admiralty pilots) are in a sense the last relic of empire. Britannia rules the waves and all that. For which you need charts and pilot books. Which is why, now and again, you get glimpses, HMS *Bossington*, for example, so what you hold in your hands is not only a pilot book, but a piece of history. Our history what is more. From Cook to Nelson to this day. If that does not sound too extravagant a claim.

17.40 Wind NE ½, Log 10, tidal set half ebb DR/Fix Aguillones bears 210. Other. I reef, square, very slow.

'Square.'

Meaning the square sail. That wonder of ancient technology. Spruce yard more than twice the beam. I remember making that. First find your spruce. Which you track down in the—here we go again—last wooden yacht building yard in Galicia. Which is down in Vigo. Proper gents they are. Building proper yachts, not very often now. You spend an agreeable morning chewing the cud with Alfredo of *Astilleros Lagos* before loading a baulk of this lovely timber and shaping, shaping, shaping. How?

You start with a square. You decide on a taper, say five inches at the centre, three and a half at the extremities. Lay on a batten and scribe a curve sweet to the eye. (There are more scientific methods in, for example, *Boatbuilding* by Howard I. Chapelle 1941—no GRP then). This on two opposing sides. Plane to the curve. Repeat batten, curve, plane, on the other two sides. Make a spar gauge. Mark on the four now tapering sides. Plane again. You now have eight sides. At this point run a pencil spiral fashion round the spar, this enables you, as the timber is removed, to keep track. Continue to sixteen and thirty-two sided and you are almost there. The rest is the sweat of your brow, hand sanding. A very satisfying process. As remembered. Don't take as gospel.

And very handsome, glistening with who knows how many coats of the best marine varnish.

Next find a sailmaker prepared to take you seriously. For a large square sail on a 28ft gaff cutter is not a common sight. But at last you do. In Cornwall. Kindred spirit, David by name, lovely man, plays music with Pete. And then of course you must wait. You do not hurry a master of his art. 'But a square sail makes a boat roll horribly.' Yes and no. Yes, on its own. No with a reef or two in the mainsail, which explains the entry *1 reef, square,* for by keeping the main, you damp the rolling. And you pick up speed, my goodness you pick up speed. This, by the way, is intended, one day, maybe, as a (speak it softly), trade wind sail.

How do you set it?

Answer: three halyards. The spar stays aloft, lifts, braces, and all.

Next log entry.

19.20. Wind NE 2. Visibility. Poor. 1 hour ebb to go. Aguillones bears 120.

Still with the Aguillones in sight, the most spectacular set of pinnacle rocks you are ever likely to see, but visibility going. This is proving to be a long, long day, and you are not even half way. You could call this nothing weather and you would not be wrong. But that is typical of this coast, it either blows holy smoke one way or ditto the other or, as now, goes all quiet, pending, as you know, the next little blow. But there is nothing you can do about it, so sit back and enjoy.

Which is exactly what we do.

For at last, the more the wind rises, the more the mist forms and the more evening draws in. And the more *Sauntress* is into her stride. Passage making, proper passage making. Which means pilotage. Yes, you can see the coast now, but not for much longer you suspect. Take some bearings, mark your position on the chart and prepare for nightfall.

'One hippopotamus, two hippopotamus.'

I beg your pardon?

'Oh, that is the way we count seconds here.'

Which is how you identify lights. As any mariner will know. And whatever else you might say about this coast, there is no shortage of lights, big powerful lights. And tonight, we are going to need them. The interesting question is whether they will be powerful enough to pierce the increasing gloom, for the mist is thickening, *Sauntress* now has a bone in her teeth, square sail straining, (think Montagu Dawson) on that grey and foam flecked eve.

'Are you sure Luis you can get the sail down at night in this wind?'

'Of course, I can.'

Silly question. *Such* a good crew.

The other preparations had been made long before we set out. Lay out your courses on the passage charts. Corrected for this and that. Now the distances. Next, on a separate sheet, the names and characteristics of the lights. Makes life so much easier. Two torches, one big and powerful. One small, that for reading the Walker trailing log. Fill the cabin oil lamp, light and turn down low. Make sure crew is warmly dressed, oilskins on, harness on, lifelines attached. Eat before sunset and have chocolate to hand.

Yes, the lights still pierce the gloom, but it is touch and go now. And a star to steer her by? No, not here. That is for offshore work, watch upon watch. But I have done it. Often. And on a moonless night there is no better way. But remember the heavens wheel.

Now we will leave *Sauntress* and her crew for the moment, as she roars, under square sail into the night, much in store for them yet, for a little spot of something else.

6

Boatbuilding, Galician Fashion

Many years ago, a certain magazine published an article entitled 'A Dinghy for Beginners' written, with his tongue firmly in his cheek, I suspect, by one Will Stirling. For Will knows perfectly well, as do I, that clinker, or lapstrake as our friends across the water call it, is, in the words of Howard I. Chapelle (op cit. p 453) *in some ways the severest test of the builder's craftsmanship and sense of proportion.*

Be that as it may, the thing had the sweetest lines imaginable, was absolutely traditional and was begging to be built. So, the best investment ever, the plans duly arrived, a workshop built, trestles made, the moulds set up and off we went in search of timber.

Well, wooden boatbuilding here is to all intents and purposes dead, with exceptions as we have seen. But there is plenty of timber around, Galicia being 'Green Spain.' Oak they use as firewood. Of mahogany the suggested timber was there none, or not at a price an ordinary mortal could afford. And in any case, when in Rome…

Pine. Knot-free pine.

Oh, what fun and games we had, but in the end, we tracked down at the back of beyond and then some, a proper Galician, speaking a slow, deep, riddled with double meanings, *gallego*, who ran a sawmill of astounding antiquity and very doubtful health and safety precautions. Gave him the patterns (stem, forefoot and so on).

'I will see what I can do. Come back in a few days.'

Imagine (as they say), my surprise when returning to find that not only had he found the timber, oak, with the sweeping grain, but he had made the stem, forefoot etc, exactly to the plans. All I had to do was assemble. Cheating really. Not my fault Guv. Promise.

'How much?'

'Gurgle, gurgle, gurgle.'

'Sorry, what did you say?'

'Gurgle, gurgle.' Must learn *gallego*.

'He is saying Martin, that you do not owe him anything.'

'Thank you, Luis.'

And what exactly is one supposed to do with that? Answer we took him a *jamón* (ham). To his bemusement. So many times, has that happened here.

We beavered away some more. Backbone finished.

Now for the pine. Up the hill from where we lived was a very different outfit. Again, a sawmill, but this one on a commercial scale, weighbridge, huge lorries, giant machinery, log after log shovelled mechanically into some machine, stack upon stack of timber, all pine. Well we knew them and they us. And they tolerated with good grace our trespassing on what was strictly a wholesale business, wood by the lorry load type operation.

'What we are looking for, Pepe, is knot-free pine.'

'What dimensions, Martin?'

As I said, they knew us.

You explain. 'Ah yes, we keep this for the bote builders,' meaning small punts. Aha, so there is boatbuilding timber. He leads us to a stack, which he demolishes in search of the very best pieces, nothing too much trouble once again.

'What dimensions?' she asks at the weighbridge. You tell her. She names a figure. So ludicrously small you ask her to repeat.

And so it went on.

I pass over the struggles with Howard Chapelle's *test of craftsmanship*, for it was just that. Particularly since in a fit of self-flagellation I chose to use hand tools only. No electric anything. Now we were left with one, or the last but one, expedition into the wilds to find oak for the top strake and the ribs. Mr *Jamón* unable to oblige this time, we found yet another antiquated operation where as we arrived, in the driving sleet, it so happened they were cutting an oak tree into planks.

You leave with your green oak having handed over a few coins of small change.

Now crooks. Luis' cousin was cutting down apple trees. And apple crooks are perfect for knees.

Which is pretty much how you build a boat in Galicia.

Thanks, Will, the boat is brilliant. And so, with all the questions were you.

Of course it went through the door.

7

Hello Darkness My Old Friend

> 2.18. Caution. Many of the lights on this coastline are placed at such elevations as to be frequently obscured by mist; the mariner may therefore have little warning of their proximity.
>
> *West Coast of Spain and Portugal Pilot. NP67*

Quite so. And it is still closing in.

But you are confident of your DR. You have almost run your distance by guestimate. (Guestimate because for some curious reason I had handed the Walker log, much more accurate than you might think, and virtually infallible, way back. Thus, depriving ourselves of that old friend). The next and last big headland is Cabo Prior. Once past that you can alter course south. There is a light way off the port bow, which is where it should be, but try as you might you cannot identify the light for sure, one hippopotamus, two hippopotamus notwithstanding.

Too much of the fluffy stuff in the atmosphere.

Luis pipes up.

'That is the Torre de Hercules' (Corunna).

'It can't be Luis, too far.'

'I am telling you it is. Don't you think I know the Torre de Hercules when I see it!'

Which vehement assertion from this Galician son of the soil, casts doubt. He could just be right. Perhaps we have we passed Cabo Prior unseen in the gloom? Yielding, and against your better judgement, you put up the helm and head south. No, that is not quite fair to Luis. For having been persuaded that the light you can see is the Torre de Hercules you become accomplice. It is a well-known phenomenon. Against all logic you make all you see fit that one idea and block out what does not fit. Of course, it is the Torre de Hercules. Only it is not. Ships have been lost like that. But now shore lights are beginning to appear where no shore lights should be. Time for technology, kept for just such an eventuality as this. Heave to and let the Garmin settle the argument.

Resume the original course.

Moral.

Tiredness kills. Take a break. (Road sign, A303).

Except here, you can't.

You stand on, well on, for the wind has backed as it strengthened from NE to NNE or thereabouts which will put you on a run. And you don't want that and an accidental gybe. And there is another small pilotage problem. The next light, Priorino Chico, marking the entrance to the Ría de Ferrol is obscured on this course. Which leaves you with a nasty spit to pile up on, should you misjudge things.

So, you stand on further to open things up, familiar lights appearing now, mist lifting at last, just to make sure. But it is odd, that light, for any vessel bound for the Ría de Ferrol, coming down from Cabo Prior (technology aside) faces the same problem, an unlit headland, unlit that is until you clear it. When it is rather too late to be useful.

Well that was interesting Luis.

Home? Well actually no. Because as we pass into the shadow of Priorino Chico and open up the *Puerto Exterior de Ferrol*, Aeolus throws a switch. No wind. You would think that in the small hours, the *ría* would be deserted. On the contrary it is filled with a swarm of fireflies, alias small boats fishing and suddenly zooming hither and thither at high speed in search, Luis informs me, of *choco*, all most disconcerting. And I don't trust their lookout an inch. On the *qui vive* again.

But not half as disconcerting as what comes next.

For something gigantic is on the move. Tug assisted. Floodlit. What on earth are they up to at this time of night? For Ferrol, the *Puerto Exterior* is not exactly a busy place. In fact, practically moribund. Coal for As Pontes and that is about it. But there it is. You are becalmed. You are in the way. And something must be done. *Restricted in ability to manoeuvre* flashes through your mind. Time for the big torch. On the sails. It works, or appears to work, for the procession slows. A puff comes, heaven be praised and at last, at last, we are clear of the nonsense and racing for home in flat waters, as light suffuses the eastern sky.

You round the final islet, El Mourón they call it.

And again, no wind. But there seldom is here.

Scull the last cable or so.

And pick up the mooring and that Will Stirling dinghy.

In at 10.30. 26½ hours.

We are back in Galicia again. The land of…

8

Fires from a Pagan Past

Certain persons have told me that if you are of a prying disposition, now is the time to observe amorous couples walking hand in hand into the gloom—passionate young lovers from different villages, who have looked forward to this night of all the year on the chance of meeting, at last, in a fervent embrace under the friendly beeches. These same stern men (they are always men) declare that such nocturnal festivals are a disgrace to civilization; that the Greek Comedy, long ago, reprobated them as disastrous to the morals of females--that they were condemned by the Council of Elvira, by Vigilantius of Marseilles and by the great Saint Jerome, who wrote that on such occasions no virgin should wander a hand's-breadth from her mother. They wish you to believe that on these warm summer nights, when the pulses of nature are felt, and senses stirred with music and wine and dance, the Gran Madre di Dio is adored in a manner less becoming Christian youths and maidens, than heathens celebrating mad orgies to Magna Mater in Daphne, or the Babylonian groves (where she was not worshipped at all--though she might have been).

In fact, they insinuate that...

It may well be true. What were the moralists doing there?

Festivals like this are relics of paganism and have my cordial approval. We English ought to have learnt by this time that the repression of pleasure is a dangerous error. In these days when even Italy, the grey-haired cocotte, has become tainted with Anglo-Pecksniffian principles, there is nothing like a little time-honoured bestiality for restoring the circulation and putting things to rights generally. On ethical grounds alone—as safety-valves—such nocturnal feasts ought to be kept up in regions such as these, where the countryfolk have not our 'facilities.' Who would grudge them these primordial joys, conducted under the indulgent motherly eye of Madonna, and hallowed by antiquity and the starlit heavens above?

Norman Douglas. Old Calabria. 1915

Not sure that *'nothing like a little time-honoured bestiality'* would pass muster nowadays, (though isn't there is something about Welsh mountain sheep?), but no matter. A broad-minded reprobate, mischievously approving of paganism, contemptuous of humbug, and a sense of humour to boot. A Presbyterian Scot and all.

A touch of the Satyr. Like here. Midsummer Nights' Dream, the *Noche de San Juan. Passionate young lovers from different villages.* That pagan festival. But everything seems strangely pagan here, pagan mixed with religion at its most fervent. Or, as Aubrey F. G. Bell puts it, *the religion of the Galician is essentially a survival of ancestor worship and revolves around the cult of the souls.* (*Spanish Galicia.* John Lane, The Bodley Head Limited, 1922).

'Here Martin, this is for you. Protects against the evil eye.'

It is Miguel speaking, the half mad and entrancing artist, who took me under his wing that first summer. For as the only Irishman (or is it Englishman?) in the place, who has turned up from the sea, in an old wooden boat, you are the subject of endless curiosity, not to say generosity. And Miguel, albeit pursued by his insanely jealous lover/agent, a perfect guide to the underbelly of Old Corunna. So, this scene takes place in a disreputable and alluring bar, TBO by name. (Later, rather unsportingly, shut down by the authorities).

And what he has just given me, as a gesture of rather conspiratorial friendship, for we are somewhat on the run, (that lover/agent), is a *figa*, the amulet with clenched fist, thumb between index and middle fingers, a talisman, to be worn around the neck, or as a bracelet.

Come Easter week and what looks like the Ku Klux Klan processes around the streets of Old Corunna. You retreat until they have passed. For the fervour is rather intimidating to one from northern climes, where *more tea Vicar?* church fêtes and the harvest festival are pretty much it. In any case for every over devout adherent to the Church of Rome, there is another, of the anarchist bent.

Rumblings of history.

'How about joining us for a *queimada?*'

And what, you wonder, are you letting yourself in for this time? Answer, take a large earthenware bowl of *licor de hierbas*, add sugar, lemon peel, cinnamon and coffee beans, heat, set fire to the potion, turn down the lights, and pour the flaming contents into *cuncas*, little earthenware tumblers, reciting (increasingly drunken) incantations against witches. Not quite *heathens celebrating mad orgies*, but then again. A memorable afternoon, that is for sure. So far, that is, as you can remember anything.

The summer solstice approaches. An awful lot of activity. Old furniture, pallets, branches, they are building a bonfire, or rather bonfires, everywhere. The market is suddenly festooned with bunches of herbs. You can't find those for the rest of the year, unless it be the ubiquitous and boring parsley. What is all this about?

San Juan. The pagan festival par excellence. Norman Douglas would have a field day. For all nature stirs on this night, witches abroad, magic at its most powerful and most dangerous. Which is why you need those herbs. For each has a property: effective against demons, protects from the evil eye, potent for love (very much in the air), but double-edged some of these, for what protects can be turned, by a witch, to nefarious purposes. So be careful. You put out the precious pot of herbs steeped in spring water, or sea water, if by the sea, to catch the night air. *No* you are corrected, not to catch the night air, *to catch the moon*. Of course, the moon. Silly me.

And by morning you have a powerful magic potion, in which to wash your face, giving eternal youth, curing all ills and, flung at your enemies, highly effective. *Aguas santas* says the Church. But to little avail. For all this is much older.

Soon, the climax. The *hogueras*.

In every town, every village, every hamlet, every household almost, the *hogueras* blaze, the wine flows, the twigs crackle and hiss. Sardines. You must have sardines. And potatoes roasted in the embers. The stinging smoke, the last rays of the sun are gone. The bonfires flare. The young lads begin the ritual. The bravest first. The flames have subsided. The embers glow. The heat hits you still. The first leap, arms flying, the whoop of joy. Sparks fly. And the night has begun. Nine times, nine times you must jump that fire. The circle of faces, around the flames, yelling encouragement, the elders remembering youth, cigar glowing, brandy in hand, shadows in the night, forms whirl in the gloom. Over the flames. Nine times. Again, and again, and again. Ever more hectic. Warm caressing night air. Stars above. A kind of madness. The longest day. Sacred since time began. No wonder *passionate young lovers*, for all stirs on this night of nights.

Which is why, here every year, in our valley, the *hoguera* blazes, the young leap and whoop whilst we, the elders, look on, nursing our brandy, in a haze of alcoholic approval. Stuffed with sardines. Under that night sky.

Up in the hills however, hang a bunch of ferns next to the ears of your horse and you keep the devil at bay. 'Yes' says Luis, 'in Lugo.' Really? Yes, it would seem so. Me, I would keep clear of such places. A little too much inbreeding. The ruined villages. You may buy one for next to nothing. The romantic escapist dream. The reality is harsher. Winter snows. Perpetual rain. And above all the Galician version of *Manon des Sources*. For should you have the ill fortune to fall out with your neighbour, the *campesino*, jealous of his land, of his rights and above all of money… You stand not a chance.

As in the disappearing Dutchman.

Much safer at sea.

9

At Close Quarters in Ferrol

First, let's see what the Admiral says:

Ría de Ferrol.
    3. 71. In the narrows, between Castillo de San Felipe (43°28′N, 8°15′W) and Punta Redonda, the tidal streams tend to follow the direction of the channel and attain a maximum rate at springs of about 4 knots. The tidal streams in both directions set towards Punta Leiras, off which they cause a rip.

West Coast of Spain and Portugal Pilot. NP67

Adding, *very heavy squalls in winter.*
But that is the nature of the place. A windy old gulch. Steep hills on both sides, tortuous channel, strong tides, and now and again, to enliven proceedings, a ship.

'Would you like a tow, Martin?'

'No *gracias*, thank you all the same.'

'See you later.'

For they, like us, are on their way to the *Parrocheira*.

Partly it is vanity, but mostly it is because I enjoy the challenge. Anyway, we are a sailing yacht pure and simple, so I prefer it that way. The initial approach is between the harbour wall of the *puerto exterior*, which extends south and which you leave to port, and the long spit extending northwards from Punta de Segano, marked by a difficult to spot starboard hand buoy. It is here, before you reach the narrows proper that you can take the measure of the squalls coming down from the heights above and decide what sail to carry. For once committed there is no room to reef.

You elect all plain sail, for you will need the power to cheat the tide. Using those sudden and fierce squalls to make up to windward. Judging to a nicety how far to stand in, take her through the eye of the wind, chase it round as it veers or backs, mind the buoys, for the tide is powerful, and slowly but surely you make ground. Exhilarating stuff, smart tacking, *this* is what we came for. And here is a thing. The jib and foresail being small, compared to say *Martlet* with her big genoa, short tacking is a pleasure. Release the sheets from the jam cleats as you come through the eye of the wind, and you have them sheeted in again in the twinkling of an eye. Like a dinghy. Agile and alive. Which is why I love this game.

Reach Castillo San Felipe, dominating the narrows to port and we are nearly there. It is here the tide runs hardest. And here you *want* a squall, to send you, lee rail under, foaming upwind and out of the clutches of the tide. It comes. You clear Castillo de Palma to starboard and you are through into *one of the best natural harbours in Spain,* says the Admiral. A naval base.

Now comes the interesting bit.

The *Parrocheira* is held in an inner basin adjoining the naval dockyard. To reach which you must sail into the dock entrance, perhaps half a cable wide, down to the bottom and then, to starboard, you have the inner basin, disused except for the tripper boat and find somewhere to bring up. Pete has preceded you, so at least there will be somebody to take your lines. Not the kind of place I would normally want to be, but there we are.

You start preparing. Warps at the ready. Fenders likewise. Furl the foresail. Leave the jib. This leaves the foredeck clear. Have the peak and throat halyards ready to run. Heaving line handy. Send Luis up forward, warp in hand, ready to throw. A look around to see what might be happening, anybody in the way?

No.

You stand in. The wind immediately plays tricks around the buildings, as expected and heads you. Well there is just room to tack, so you do. The wind whips round again. Back on a reach. Start to slow the boat, by easing off the peak, (remember the topping lift first), rucking the main. Ah! there is Pete. Good. Stand on, for you are judging, as with picking up the mooring, how far you will carry your way.

'Ready.'

Helm down, shoot up into the wind, quick now, before it changes.

'Now Luis!'

And Pete catches the line.

We are in.

Tonight, we will visit our favourite restaurant in a narrow alley (always avoid the harbour-front places), post speeches by worthies in a marquee, free T-shirts, and all the jollification which comes with such events. Poor Ferrol. Both Geraldine and I are entranced and depressed by turns by the beauty and neglect of the old town. The usual problem. No-one wants those old houses. But we have not come sight-seeing, we have come to eat a jolly good meal and celebrate a challenging and rewarding day.

Next morning you have it all to do again, sail out, parade with the rest, sail in again and party. And that is it. You hobnob, admire other people's boats (*vela tradicional*) chew the cud until the early hours aboard Martlet and wake, bleary eyed, on the morrow.

So what wind have we got today? Westerly by the look of it. September weather. You warp the boat round to face into the wind. Tuck a reef into the mainsail against eventualities. And leave the sail set. Single up. Now set and back the jib. Cast off forward, giving a good shove and the ship will pivot on the after warp. 'Cast off Pete' and *Sauntress* gathers way. There is the head of the quay opposite to clear, after which you tidy up, set the foresail, and breathe easy.

'See you next year.'

Yes, indeed. See you next year.

Well, that anchorage. Most of the *ría* past the narrows is pretty bleak and industrial with nowhere enticing to anchor. Except this one spot. Which is tucked in behind Castillo de Palma, out of the tide and the fairway, a little bay, a sandy beach, trees, a kind of hideaway. With the added bonus, particularly for Luis, of being an easy walk to Mugardos, the *pulpo* mecca. And opposite the Castillo San Felipe and La Graña, and the heights above.

And where now and again, you can watch the astonishing spectacle of the bows of a very large ship emerging, slowly revealing itself, thump, thump, from behind the Castillo de Palma. And should you feel so inclined, speculate on the impregnability of the place.

Witness this curious paragraph under the resonant title: *The Monthly Magazine. Or British Register. Volume 11—State of Public Affairs in February, 1801, p179:*

> Respecting the failure of the Ferrol expedition the following facts have appeared and as a matter of authentic information we submit them to our readers. The expedition having arrived off Ferrol Sir J. B. Warren informed Sir R. Abercrombie that it would be extremely practical to destroy the whole of the enemy's fleet in that harbour if the troops would first silence the batteries of Fort St Philip [Castillo San Felipe] which could not be approached by our shipping. 12,500 men were accordingly landed under the direction of Sir Edward Pellew who displayed uncommon judgement in superintending the disembarkation as not even a musket was lost in this service. [At which point appears a footnote 'a transport with 400 troops was however, run down by a man of war, and every man on board perished'. Hum]. The landing being effected, the troops were marched up the hill which overlooks fort St Philip without opposition from the enemy who fled in great consternation into Ferrol, where all the churches were opened to hear mass and to beseech the protection of the saints. It was expected that the signal to advance would be given without delay; when to the surprise of every part of the service, the troops were ordered to retrace their ground and re-embark.

As for the failure that is true enough. As for *fled in consternation into Ferrol, where all the churches were opened to hear mass and beseech the protection of the saints,* this, according to the Spanish sources, is a gross calumny. Yes, it was a saint's day (always is here), but no, far from fleeing in consternation, the local militia and irregulars, though badly outnumbered, harassed the advancing troops (the guerrilla tactics later used so successfully against Napoleon), to such effect that the assault was called off. Indeed the self-same Napoleon, then Spain's ally, went so far as to raise a glass to *los valientes ferrolanos.* But, equally plausibly, to resume *The Monthly Magazine. Or British Register Volume 11—State of Public Affairs:*

> The reason assigned by the most respectable authority, for this counter order, was the determination of a council of war, which was of the opinion that it would not be practicable to take fort St Philip without risking the loss of 3000 men, and that to attack it in a regular way, would require eight days before the last parallel could be completed; that this delay would be dangerous on many accounts, as, besides the re-enforcements that might be sent to Ferrol, there would be a great risk from a change of wind, which might drive our fleet off the coast and leave our army in the same situation that it was at Ostend.

The temptation to explore what happened at Ostend resisted, the fact was that the fleet was anchored in an open roadstead between Cabo Prior and Cabo Priorino Chico, completely exposed to any wind with a westerly component. Which in turn leads one to wonder quite how they managed naval manoeuvres if not naval warfare in those times. Not always, to judge by the running down of the unfortunate transport, quite as deftly as we are led to suppose. The answer is to be found in *The elements of rigging, seamanship and Naval tactics.* Published 1794. David Steel. The authoritative work of the time. Essential reading for every midshipman worth his salt.

And invaluable, presumably, to the likes of Patrick O'Brian.

To take an enemy ship by boarding, from the lee for instance, is described (having first cleared for action), in the following passage. Imagine, for a moment, a pursuit, *Master and Commander* style, for he has chased down his adversary at last. He does not need the textbook. But we do. And we must pay attention. For this is nothing if not seamanship. Seamanship in the age of sail. And something of a source of wonderment.

> In order to execute this manoeuvre, the boarder is to come within pistol shot, close in the wake, or, at most, to the weather quarter of the ship he means to attack; taking care to continue steering, so as not to be raked by any of the guns which belong to the quarter he stands on. Then, to come up with his adversary, he must edge away a little, and range round aft, so close upon the enemy's lee quarter, that his cat-head may almost touch her quarter gallery. Now, when you have shot sufficiently a-head, your ship being parallel to your adversary's, so as to bring your forecastle abreast of your enemy's mainmast, the mizzen and mizzen staysail sheets are to be hauled well aft, the helm put hard a-lee, and the head sheets let fly; then, your ship, coming rapidly to the wind (§ 44, 50, & 31), [these numbers are paragraph numbers describing the handling of a ship in a particular circumstance] shivers her sails, and closes the opposing vessel side to side. This manoeuvre is infallible when you have the advantage of sailing, [meaning if your vessel is faster] provided very great attention is paid to it. But great attention is necessary; because, if at this moment the weather ship, which wishes to avoid the boarding, either sets her courses, [the lowest and largest of the tier of square sails on a given mast], or lays all those flat a-back which she had set, she may perchance break the grapnels if you have neglected to trim your sails in the same manner as hers: for, by making more sail, if the wind be a little fresh, she will shoot a-head through the water, and drag the boarder with such force as to break the chains or hawsers by, which the two ships are confined together. By laying all flat to the mast, the boarded vessel is still more likely to succeed, since the sails of one ship will be full, while those of the other are a-back.
>
> This mode of boarding may, as shewn before, be anticipated and avoided, if the boarder does not pay the strictest attention to his own as well as to his adversary's manoeuvres: but it may be still more readily avoided; if the last mentioned vessel braces her head sails sharp a-back, setting only, if neces-

> sary, the fore sail (§ 37), at the same instant laying to the mast or shivering (according to the necessity for more or less sternway) all those which are abaft, (§ 36.) and putting the helm hard a-lee (§ 58). All this is to be executed when the boarder is still about a ship's length (more or less) a-stern of the other vessel. The quickness of this evolution, and the rapid veering of the weather ship, may bring the boarding vessel, which is a little to leeward or a-stern of the other, into the most dangerous situation, if she does not manoeuvre in the same manner and with equal celerity; as the boarder's sails, being full, keep up his velocity, and may, before he can veer, engage his bowsprit in the main shrouds of the enemy, who pays short round on her head.

A touch of the Lewis Carroll about this passage, *Then the bowsprit got mixed with the rudder sometimes* (The Hunting of the Snark).

> This terrible and dangerous situation is infinitely to be dreaded; and it is of the highest importance to pay the strictest attention to your own manoeuvres, and to those of your opponent, which you are to endeavour to foresee and avoid as much as possible.

Now, should you wish to make *Fire Hoops, Fire arrows and Lances*, or *Thunder powder, Stink Balls*, or an *Artificial Earthquake*, or *Combustible Composition for Destroying objects or giving alarm*, or *a fire pot that cannot be extinguished by water*, then you need *Marshall's Practical Marine Gunnery*, United States Navy 1822.

Who said history was boring?

10

Redes Regatta

Lovely word, regatta. Bucolic. Putting one in mind of the village fête of old. Flags, bunting, buns and a good old midsummer hop. Or a roll in the hay.

Redes regatta has something of that flavour. Once a year it brings together craft, not just from Redes, but from the surrounding waterside villages, Ares, Sada and further afield. Ferrol and Corunna for example. The spirit of the regatta is the *vela tradicional*, or traditional sail. The surviving working boats from earlier times. *dornas*, whose true home is around Cape Finisterre, the *rías baixas*, the design Scandinavian influenced, two-man craft, not exactly stable, built to fish, out on the land breeze, back on the sea breeze; the *botes*, slightly larger, again built for fishing, rigged like the *dorna* with the *vela relinga*, which is an early form of standing lug-sail.

And plenty of characters besides.

Pepe Osorio for one. Whose open boat, festooned with such things as a candle in a bottle for a navigation light, he had taken around Cape Finisterre, an astonishingly adventurous voyage and who, whatever the weather, would be out. Not of the ruling class he, for his politics, like the politics of so many, is rooted in the 1930s and that piece of Spanish history. And who on the occasion of Sauntress' centenary, was the only boat, other than *Sauntress*, to be out on the water. For a storm came. The regatta was cancelled. We sailed the course, out of bravado, with Pepe Osorio showing us how. And he a grandfather and all.

And Picaño. The genuine article. House by the water. A quiet, wise and dignified man. Above politics, be it village or otherwise. He has three boats, a little *bote*, a *lancha* and a small yacht he built for his son, to a design taken from a magazine, years back. All kept immaculately in a livery of white picked out in red. Every year, each one in turn is hauled up on the slip. He puts on his working clothes, runs a cable from his front window to the slip, such is the view from his house, brings his box of tools, little ship-wrighting jobs, sand, paint, antifoul. And back onto the moorings, trim and gleaming they go. And for how many years has he been doing that? More than he would care to remember, I suspect.

And to him, mentally, you doff your hat.

Ashore the stage is set. Literally so. For the prize giving and the music which follows in the evening. Barbecues are prepared. Sardines, sausages, bread. The smoke stinging the eyes. And yes, there is bunting. And rockets to announce the *fiesta*.

Out on the water and by the slip, last minute preparations, tangles to untangle, sails bent, a good deal of banter. An eye on the weather too. With luck the usual northeaster. And the setting?

A kind of amphitheatre. Redes looks out eastward to the head of the *ría*. Into which flows the river Eume. Under what they call the iron bridge, which carries the railway. To left and right, wooded hills. Which make for fluky winds, sudden squalls and then nothing, until the next one. As good a setting as you could wish for, both for the participants and the watchers on shore.

Then there is the needle match. All serious.

Cutlasses between teeth, as our rival *El Portugués* puts it. The *El Portugués* because he works in Vigo, which is Portugal as far as Redes is concerned.

His boat, named *Abur*, meaning goodbye, as in 'catch me if you can', is a modified *bote del Eo*, built by Pacho to *El Portugués'* specification. Which is to say he took the traditional fishing boat design, added a fin keel and bulb ballast, slapped on a deck and cabin, and added a gaff cutter rig. Which makes her fast. Skimming dish fast. Something about wetted surface.

But we are fast too. In fact, despite the difference in boats, for *Sauntress* is a traditional long keeled gaff cutter dating from 1913, there is little to choose between the two in terms of racing performance. Which gives the watchers ashore a kind of bonus, the regatta proper and the private feud, *Sauntress* and *Abur*.

So, they set up a curtain raiser, the day before the regatta, called the *desafío Irlanda/Redes*, where the two of us could slug it out over several hours. Zipping around the amphitheatre but out to Ares as well. As many circuits as we could fit in before the wind went, two circuits usually.

'Make sure you win today, Martin.' There is money on it.

'Whatever you do don't get involved in a luffing match.'

And other such admonitions.

Which at first sight is odd, rooting for the outsider. But the explanation lies in part in the hierarchy of the village, 'airs and graces' versus quite the opposite, Chus for example could never be said to have 'airs and graces'. Others most definitely did. Add to the mix long nursed grievances, the politics of left and right, which given history, means rather more than the simple words might suggest and of course there will be factions. *El Portugués* belonging, by default to what one might call the upper class of Redes. And *El Irlandés* by adoption, to another.

Peasant versus gentry if you like. Which made it that much more entertaining for all concerned. The undercurrents of village life writ large on the water. Opposite which, high on the escarpment stands the Castillo de Andrade, a medieval fortress, witness to peasant versus gentry on a massive scale, *Los Irmandiños*, the 15th century uprising in Galicia and beyond. Like Watt Tyler, and his peasants revolt. And for fundamentally the same reasons. And it is remembered. And turned into an annual *fiesta*. Any excuse for one of those.

Peasant versus gentry. That certainly resonates here.

Redes was a fishing village. Like so many. Very simple. Very picturesque in its way, but poor. Not anymore. Now it rejoices in such titles as *The Venice of Galicia*. There was however one last fisherman, Chus by name, who, like his father and grandfather before him, fished, commercially. It is a messy, cold business, dead of night laying of pots. Dragging plastic buckets of bait through the sea of visitors to the *Venice of Galicia* (what nonsense), strangely alien in his own village, coarse, loud mouthed, but what you saw was what you got with Chus. And for that I liked him. He is gone now, carried off by whatever the doctors say, but in my view, of a broken heart.

The price of progress and all that rubbish.

It is all very well, Benito, but I enjoy a luffing match. So, does *El Portugués* and so, most definitely do the spectators. Medieval jousting, (to continue the analogy), bowsprit for sword. Duck and weave. Try this way. Try that. Catch him by surprise. He looks back, all anxious, which is the idea. We both relished the close quarters stuff, the closer the better. Blood up. Momentary lapse on *El Portugués'* part and you have him.

Not easy though, canny old bastard was *El Portugués*.

Which made winning all the sweeter. We are gone now.

But not before claiming one last time, the coveted double, the *Desafio* and the Regatta. *Abur.*

11

Three Men in a Boat

'**M**artin, I think this is meant for you.'

It was. The missive had bounced around the ether in Redes before finally landing where intended. A *cri de coeur* and best of all, a proper passage beckons. You crossed Biscay way back, since when you have fiddled. But now you have a new challenge.

For the boat is twenty feet plus an inch or two long, is unknown, as is the writer of the missive, and this boat is in a place you need to look up, called Bourgenay on the west coast of France. The flat boring bit. You ask what you trust are the right questions. Get what seem the right answers. Muster an extra crew, one David. And set off into the unknown.

For all the world as though on the hippy trail. Clutching this and that (charts for one thing). And like any true hippy you fall on your feet rather. Wined and dined in fine style, a bit goggle-eyed at the splendour of the setting—big stone house in the countryside, you go through the motions of preparing this vessel for sea.

It is new. You can see that. It is a gaff cutter. It was built by her father, in a barn. And it is utterly engaging. The term Caroline's father used—for the writer is Caroline and this is how we met—is *slow and obstinate like me*.

So off we go into the blue yonder, complete with a silver ladle purloined with Caroline's connivance, from her eagle-eyed *maman*, a *daube*, a lot of tobacco and plenty of porridge. And quite possibly a runcible spoon.

In command of the good ship *Eltoraji*.

Her first trick is to sail backwards. Because she is on the heavy side. There is little wind. And is a so-and-so to steer. So, when you are not looking, she sneaks up into the wind, hesitates and starts sailing backwards.

The days pass, relatively uneventfully, slightly erratic course as the weather tries to decide what to do. You exhaust the *daube* and move on to I cannot remember what. Luis is in charge of the galley. Which is a one-burner camping gas, in a kind of cupboard, where, pot balanced precariously, Luis is on his knees. Ablutions are bucket and chuck it. Until, well it had to happen didn't it, rather more than a hatful of wind.

And off she goes like a startled faun.

Grey and horrible and all rather exciting.

The old game. How much wind? Answer, I have no idea. Three reefs and foresail weather, five knots or more across some remarkably steep seas. (There is a GPS to tell you that kind of thing). Conditions which suit *Eltoraji* well. Switchback ride, spray everywhere, Luis trussed like a chicken to the weather rail, for the motion is violent. Violent enough to pitch you overboard. A game little ship. Crew hanging on as best they can. Soaking wet down below. All the usual ingredients in fact.

But it cannot last. And does not last that long. A little summer tempest.

'Land ho.'

Luis produces the longed-for porridge, forgetting to add milk or water—surreptitiously tipped overboard—and we reach our destination, Ribadeo.

At which point he discovers the beer in the bilges. And the rest is…

12

Spring is Sprung

The grass is riz,
I wonder where the birdie is?
The birdie's on the wing, ain't that a funny thing?
I always thought the wing was on the bird.
Ain't that absurd?

Sorry, I could not resist that.

Refit time. Combined with a bit of history. *El Portugués* chooses to refit in secret. In Sada. You may be sure he is up to something. He always is. It is an obsession. And, being a surgeon, he is meticulous. And all with one thing in view. To beat *El Irlandés*. Which, to give him his due, he sometimes does. It would be dull if he did not.

New mast. A beauty. Hollow, in spruce, built by *Astilleros Lagos*, down in Vigo. And more ballast to match. New fancy cut foresail. A failure. Longer bowsprit. And at last, a topsail. Which done, we are photographically speaking, two peas in a pod. Same rig, same coloured sails, same angle of heel (the hulls scarcely visible beneath this spread of canvass), for the photograph was taken from ahead, all you see is a graceful pyramid of sail, a kind of double take, the one almost superimposed on the other.

No wonder we are evenly matched.

We fit out in Ares. Hercules Marine. Paco, like any yard owner, harassed, overworked, an office of a kind, a portacabin. And Jose, his brother (there are three), who in his gloominess might as well be Eeyore. All a bit ramshackle. Which suits us.

This is part yacht yard, part working boat yard. A trawler up on the trolley and you must wait. A steel hull to sandblast. No varnishing today. Something to do with fiberglass and there they are, protective clothing.

Try not to breathe the fumes.

But easygoing.

Our materials are of the traditional kind. Jeffery's Marine glue, Glazier's putty, raw linseed oil and red lead powder, neatsfoot oil, leather, waxed twine (these last three better got from a place where they sell things for horses, more sensibly priced), underwater primer, undercoat, topcoat (off-white enamel), varnish, and elbow-grease. A lot of that.

Any owner of a wooden boat will know the process. If Luis is rubbing down the topsides once again, I will be tap, tapping, below the water line with that 'Spanish Armada' seam rake. Get rid of the loose stopping, gently now, firm up, if need be, the caulking, then, you take a tupperware box, the putty, the linseed oil and the red lead powder and, mind in neutral, you work this mix until you are satisfied. Perfectly smooth, no lumps, and the right consistency. Find your favourite spatula and apply. Allow to dry. Although now and again you take her back to bare wood, nasty job, just to check. No rot? No loose fastenings? Good. That will do for a few years yet.

Re-leather the gaff saddle. You can do that on the kitchen table. Cut the leather to size. Find a pyrex bowl. Fill with neatsfoot oil. Work the leather until soft and stitch. Here you will consult your bible on such things, *The Rigger's Apprentice*. And whilst at it, leather all else that needs leathering and there is plenty of that on a gaffer.

Or renew the running rigging. Which comes from those people in Holland who supply the tall ships.

'How many reels?'

'Well just one actually.'

You still get the discount. Which is substantial.

Every year a little project. Wooden boats are like that. Simple tools, simple materials, nothing beyond the ordinary mortal, if that mortal is, as they say back in Ireland, handy with a toolbox.

There is a history of the boat, incomplete, but revealing all the same. For when you bought the boat back in 1973 you were given the Certificate of British Registry, Part 1, in a mauve cover. You unfold the parchment, for it is parchment, and here, in copperplate, signed by the Registrar of Shipping, Lowestoft, is the history of her ownership. 64 64th shares and all.

> I hereby certify that on this 4th day of July 1955, John Massey Fuller Colonel, Royal Marines retired, of Tavistock in the County of Devon, is registered sole owner of the vessel within described.
>
> Kirkham, Registrar of Shipping
Port of Lowestoft

So, runs the first but one entry. There are ten more. You can see when she changed hands and where the owners lived, on the East Coast mostly, at times transferred twice in the same year, and never more than three years in the same ownership. The implication is obvious. There was something about her that was not quite right. But what? I cannot be sure, but I suspect the answer was she frightened people. Not able to stand up to her canvass. Too tender in other words. Certainly, that was our experience on that first voyage years ago. Give her a yachtsman's gale and she could not get up to windward. Just leant over and sulked. Which is why, later, her iron ballast keel was removed and a replacement recast in lead. A drastic, not to say expensive, step, but it did the trick.

One final thing before we launch. Those 64 64th shares. Why this? Well, here is an interesting answer. And in good old-fashioned prose at that:

FRACTIONAL SHAREHOLDING IN BRITISH MERCHANT SHIPS WITH SPECIAL REFERENCE TO 64THS

By Rupert C. Jarvis

The property in every registered British merchant ship is by law divided into 64 shares. This fact has given rise to much conjecture and many and curious are the various theories that have been advanced at one time and another to explain away this apparently arbitrary division. Where the more modest investigators have been content to find its origin in the prize practice of the Napoleonic Wars, the more ambitious have gone either south to the medieval Mediterranean, or north to the dark age Vikings. Indeed, some have succeeded in tracing it even further, not only to Classical Rome, but to early Biblical times. Up to date the best distance run has been performed by a relatively recent text-book, that went so far as Noah's Ark, which although not exactly a Registered British Merchant Ship, did display (so it seems) all the familiar features of part-ownership and the essential characteristics of this binary division of shares, at least part of the way to the familiar 64.

Love the Noah's Ark bit.

The current law is expressed in the Merchant Shipping Act of 1896. The property in a ship shall be divided into sixty-four shares. It is as simple as that.

Except:

The plain business man, the bronzed sea dog, the pale but keen-eyed lawyer and scholar will away with all such simplicity. For example, the typical current text-book of shipping business practice lays it down quite categorically that this division of a ship into 64th is not so much a division 'made by law' as it is a division 'by ancient custom'. All the law does, so it seems, is merely to recognize this 'ancient custom.'

The Mariner's Mirror, Volume 45 1959, Issue 4.

Ready at last, the trolley trundles down the slip. Ease afloat and does she leak?

Yes, a bit. Towed to the pontoon again. Let her rest. Let her take up. Top up on drinking water, from the pontoon. And wait. Up at dawn. No wind. But you know what will happen. In the afternoon the NE will set in. Strong here. And pin you. But in the morning, in settled weather, you have that southerly just for a short while. And with that you can get away.

And pick up, once again, the mooring.

13

The Night Passage

The moon had long since set.

From the cockpit came a low murmur of contented conversation, the kind that comes after a small challenge met and surmounted. For all was quiet now, a breeze off the land, smooth water, inky black night punctuated by the flash of yet another light on yet another cape, velvet sky above and the knowledge that soon enough dawn would come.

The skipper, below, nominally sleeping, smiled inwardly, absorbing the unmistakable sounds of a happy ship, before wearily rousing himself once again.

'So, you were not sleeping?'

'No, just resting my eyes.'

'Look,' said Caroline, 'I can see the Pole Star.'

The Great Bear and Cassiopeia the pointers. Milky Way in fine fettle. No shore lights to distract. A warm summers' night. One of the best. Just the occasional gust to remind of what had gone before. *Eltoraji*, for we were aboard *Eltoraji* once again, had acquitted herself well. Caroline was almost singing for the joy of the moment, Luis refusing, but refusing to sleep, lit the skipper yet another cigarette and gave a hopeful tug on the fishing line.

'What were you saying Luis?'

He is reminiscing. His days in England, a bewildering variety of jobs. And a strange predilection for Tunbridge Wells. What escapade this time, you wonder? For Luis, on these occasions, is very good value. Guaranteed to liven up a long night watch.

'The landlady, she say not unlock the drink until 11 in the morning, but why not? They like gin. You see I have key. Very old ladies.'

And you, Luis, just a bit mischievous. Those little old ladies and their gin. Antimacassars, bet there were antimacassars, and the odd aspidistra besides. Gentility. Suffocating gentility. And Luis a breath of Spanish fresh air. 'Don't tell the landlady. I open now. Alright?'

It is of course alright.

'In Bournemouth?'

'Yes, in Bournemouth.'

'And they lived there all year?'

'Yes, yes, all year.'

Well we know what that is, don't we? You can see the signs, *Mon Repos*, *Sea Breezes*, those terraces, Edwardian or Victorian, the faded face of the railway boom, the 'Great British Seaside', the pier, the cafés, the band, the pierced and the tattooed, and the Taj Mahal (steamy windows, formica tables, sticky plasticised menu), all on a wet Sunday afternoon.

But one last thing.

'And did it have sea views?'

'Did it have…?'

'Sea views, Luis, did it have SEA VIEWS?'

'Sea views, what sea views, I not understand, sea views, what sea views?'

Oh, for goodness sake, Luis, you are not Manuel.

'*Joder Luis, el mar!* The sea! *Me entiendes*, the sea.'

'Ah sí, yes, yes, it have sea views.'

'Well that's a ***** boarding house. And how they must have loved you.'

'Yes, yes, I cook for them, special dishes, Spanish.'

I bet you did. I just bet you did. What was it you said about porridge? 'In Galicia we feed it to the animals.' You are supposed, Luis, to add milk. Very Celtic, I might add. Have you never heard of Scott's Porage Oats? Sporran and all. Pretty miffed I was about that. For hot porridge, with honey and brown sugar, in a cold grey dawn, is balm to this mariner's soul. No such luck.

But a better man in a crisis, you could not wish for.

The night wore on.

Below, as always, were the Admiralty charts, the parallel rule, the pencil, the dividers, the binoculars and pencilled marks showing where we thought we were and where we ought to be going. The courses pencilled in before we left. Obstinately old fashioned in one sense. A good way to learn in another. The compass course, the last headland, low this time, El Roncadoiro Fl W 7.5 seconds 21 miles, some way off the starboard bow. And Estaca de Bares astern. A couple of bearings, a quick check on the chart. Yes, we are far enough off. For you need to be careful with El Roncadoiro, set back, as it is, quite a way from the danger it marks. Caroline calls it instinct. And in a way it is, but ingrained habit would be nearer the mark, that and listening to the ship speaking to you, easy now, chuckling along, three reefs and all.

No hurry, she is saying, no hurry.

You keep forgetting. The tides on this coast run east on the flood, west on the ebb, strength negligible. Except here. Off this headland, for the ebb sweeps around the great bay that is the Golfo de Foz, gathering strength as it does so. Quite enough to bring us to a near standstill. But such is the atmosphere aboard that nobody seems to mind. Tired or not we are in no rush to finish the passage, so the reefs are left in, the engine slumbers, GPS too, and crew banter on.

But quite how we came to be here is another matter.

We had delivered that yacht to Ribadeo, and that, it rather seemed, was that. Day sails in the *ría*, the occasional sortie a few miles up or down the coast. For Caroline was teaching herself how to sail. Getting used to the boat. Nothing too adventurous you would think.

Well, one morning she materialised in Redes, unannounced, an eighty-mile passage. In secret. Which had the desired jaw dropping effect. For that, in a twenty-foot yacht, on this coast, is by any standards adventurous. Rub your eyes and look again. Yes, that is definitely *Eltoraji* and that tall blonde figure, cycled across Africa she did. Well, blow me. She's done it again.

'*Esta mujer, sí que tiene cojones.*'

Which delightful comment means, Good God, that woman has balls. In fact, she rather wowed Redes, appearing, as she did, from nowhere, like some latter-day Viking.

But then it was time to go home. David, her crew, the world's original overgrown boy scout, short trousers and all, was called away. Which left us. We waited for the weather, which eventually came, a gentle westerly and off, with nothing much to report, we went. Luis fishing. Walker log streamed. Engine assisted, until, that is we were abreast of Punta Candelaria, where, of a sudden, the wind rose and went on rising. Two reefs became three reefs became no mainsail at all, just foresail and five and a half knots.

> 1.130. On the Coast the weather on a cold front may be greatly accentuated by the land especially in mountainous regions and can often give rise to very violent squalls...
>
> *Admiralty Pilot. NP 67*

Here we go again.

'Caroline, do you have warps aboard?'

'Yes. What for?'

'To slow the boat.'

We were seen in our struggles with thrashing canvas. A large white trawler changed course and came to investigate. Not for the first time, nor for the last, that happens. The unwritten law of the sea. Look as though you are in trouble, which we were not, but could have been, the instinctive reaction is to help. Very comforting. We waved, gave the thumbs up and they went on their way.

The squall eased. There was no more talk of warps. And the passage resumed. Which takes us to nightfall and that chit chat under the stars.

Interlude

'How did you do that?'

'No idea, Pete, honest.'

Which is the plain truth. The *that* is a trick that certain craft sometimes perform, but very rarely so. And it is one that borders on witchcraft. It is called, quite simply, sailing with no wind. In defiance, it seems of the laws of physics. Or logic, or whatever you like.

The proof of this particular pudding lies in a late September afternoon. All is still. We are on the mooring in Redes. The beach and a rock spit lie half a cable away. A yacht is moored inconveniently close. And we are due somewhere else. Which is a conundrum.

Well perhaps some wind will come. So, you hoist all sail, topsail included. The sea is glass. You try the old fag smoke trick. But no. It simply spirals upward.

Deep breath.

'Drop the mooring Luis.'

He gives you an old-fashioned look.

You see, a memory is stirring. A piece of witchcraft you saw years ago. A smack on the Swale, stealing across a glassy sea. It made such an impression at the time. Otherwise why remember? And you wonder. Could it just be?

Pete, watching, scrambles into the inflatable, putters across the intervening stretch of water and looks askance. For he thinks what I think. What if we drift onto the rocks?

You touch nothing. Just wait.

Whilst the witch takes the gentlest possible hold. *Sauntress* is beginning to pivot, bowsprit swinging, clear of the moored yacht. All sail hanging limp.

'Sit on this side Luis and don't move.'

Why so?

To give the boat a slight list, to port as it happens. You push the boom out over the quarter. Make sure the headsail sheets are free. So far you have not touched the helm, but now you bring it amidships, finger light touch and wait.

She is making way. No doubt about it. Very gently you try the tiller. Yes, she is responding. In fact, rather more than responding. She is gathering speed. Another glance at the water. Still glass.

A round of applause across the water. That yacht.

A tell-tale stirs. Not that there is any wind, except that generated by your own motion through the water. Pete, in the inflatable, can no longer keep up.

And so, you get to wherever it was you were going.

But in answer to the question. How did we do that?

'No idea Pete. Absolutely no idea.'

But fun, wasn't it?

14

On Mud Pies and Other Misadventures

'Where is the boat?'
You blink a bit and look again.
But no. There is no boat where the boat should be.

Your face, you are told later, is an absolute picture. And no wonder. Incredulity is replaced with rising panic. How can a boat, particularly *Sauntress*, simply disappear? Evaporate into the ether. Stolen? Who on earth would be able to manage her? Has she broken her mooring? If so she will be on the rocks somewhere. Nobody here seems to know anything.

What to do?

You climb into the van. And drive off on mission impossible. To find your errant vessel. A sweaty palmed hour or two of futile activity. But what else can you do? The mobile rings.

'She is in Praia de Sabadelle.'

Flood of relief. And where might that be?

Around the corner it transpires.

For *Sauntress* had gone wandering, taking her mooring block with her. A passing fishing boat had seen her, taken her in tow and being unable to make up against the perennial north-easter, had tucked her up in the next bay, anchor out, still with mooring block, and disappeared without a word.

To this day we do not know who to thank.

Moral.

Look to your ground tackle.

Strange though it might seem, it is a habit she has. She worries and frets until finally free and takes off on a little wander on her own. In Pyefleet, she ended up on a mudbank. In Ireland she ended up in a reed bed. And lesson learned, you always, but always have the line parcelled against chafe. But to lift the entire mooring? That was something new.

Off to the scrapyard for the most enormous chain imaginable. And re-enforcing bars and bags of cement, for it is mud pie time. Make a box out of deal. Puddle away, bury the end of the chain, with re-enforcing bars crosswise through the last link, all very public this. For we are on the slip, under the windows of Charo's bar, field day for the wiseacres, for you are new to this game. In Ireland they did it for you. For a consideration. Here, you are expected to do it yourself. Now you have two mooring blocks. And peace of mind.

Which is how, when Pete's turn came, you repeat the entire performance. Two blocks. And bigger for *Martlet* is thirteen tons against *Sauntress* five or so. And further out, for *Martlet* draws a good deal of water.

Now you need help.

Lever the blocks off the quay, plop, splash, the right way up, you trust. And no, you have not forgotten to attach the line.

Enter Antonio, son of Perisel, the taciturn waterman. Every proper harbour has one such. Seen it all, sceptical, eye missing nothing, Perisel's word is pretty much law. He owns several of the moorings here, looks after the summer moorings up at the head of the ría. So, when Perisel grunts his approval of your handiwork, you have, so to speak, the seal of approval.

Antonio is as outgoing as Perisel is taciturn. A rather mischievous gap-toothed grin. A bit of a lad, especially with the girls.

'After lunch Antonio?'

'After lunch.'

A thunderous roar and clouds of diesel fumes and the work boat, known to all as the *vaporetto* bursts into life. A converted lifeboat with lorry engine, just one of the odder craft on the moorings. He spins the wheel, gears grind (once the gearbox was re-conditioned, re-installed, the gear thrown into ahead, boat goes astern, red faces and a few choice words echo across the water) and with a flourish the thing is stationed above the sunken blocks.

Half tide. But making. Wait a little.

We all hop aboard for the fun.

'Here Pete?'

Pete checks his bearings. This tree lined up with that gable. This post lined up with that rock.

'That will do.'

In Ireland they did it with oil drums, *we drew lots to see who was going to cut the line.*

Here it is a slip knot.

And all are happy. Not least Antonio, who has mouths to feed.

15

Grumpy Old Men

What's that ****** racket? I turn in my bunk, trying ineffectually to block out the noise, pretending it is not daylight, head buried in the pillow. But it is no good. A thump on the deck, a kind of scuffling I cannot identify. Oh God, he is fishing again.

Time to get up and make coffee. Lift the little teak chopping board which fits neatly above the sink—rather proud of that, I am, clever use of space, for of space there is not much aboard, to find the source of the scuffle. A not quite dead fish, a good deal of scales and bloodstains. Which is the trouble with fishing, the messiest activity going.

And it is not just the fish. It is all the paraphernalia which goes with it. Rods, bait, tangles of line. And worst of all, lying in wait, those hooks. In the most unexpected places. Drawing both blood and curses.

But mustn't complain.

Fish for supper. Though two would be better.

First the coffee. An exercise in persnicketiness. Pedantic even. Left hand glass jar. Unscrew the coffee pot. A few strokes on the foot pump. Don't over-fill. Water is precious. Replace the chopping board. Now the coffee. Screw the top on. Place on the burner. Replace glass jar. Open the cool box, behind the double sink. Teak top held down by chromed clasp. Take out the milk. Now the milk pan. Next to the bigger pan. Both have their place. Cannot slip. Cannot rattle. For there is nothing more infuriating on a boat than that persistent and hard to trace intermittent sound of something loose somewhere. Usually just as you are trying to get to sleep. That obsession with order. Order down below, order on deck. It is not just that I, for one, cannot function amidst chaos. Nor, safely, can a ship. *No! The chart table is for charts. Do not leave the (kettle, plate, mug) on the companionway steps. Do not do this. Do not do that.* God, how tiresome I must be. But order. You must have order. Pour the milk, enough for two cups. Now stretch a hand into the cockpit and raise the gas bottle lid. Turn on the gas, Shut the lid. Light the rings. Take two cups from their place. Again, cannot slip. Cannot rattle. Now the sugar, next glass jar along. He takes four teaspoonfuls. I take two. Replace the jar. Glass? Yes, glass. Not plastic. Detest plastic. Why should a ship, or a holiday cottage for that matter have to do with second best, chipped mugs, mismatched cutlery, cheap cast offs? They have been aboard forty years those glass jars. That kind of persnicketiness.

Roll the first fag of the day. And whilst coffee is making, tidy up the bunk. Roll the sleeping bag. Fluff up the pillow. Reset the lee cloth. For my quarters are up in the forepeak, with the sails, the inflatable, the riding light, the chain locker, and the heads. Snug and private. Small reading light. Daylight through the porthole in the forehatch, that leak I keep meaning to fix.

He is still up there on the afterdeck, casting, casting, casting. Hour after hour. What is he thinking about?

The coffee bubbles. Ready. Switch off the gas. Reach into the cockpit and switch off at the bottle. Pour, stir, and hand out the cup.

'Coffee Luis. How's the fishing?'

Later he will gut the fish in the bucket, sluice down the cockpit and put away his tackle. Another day on the mooring has begun. All quiet this morning. Others will be out, pottering around the bay, banter, 'how many?' *'Nada.'* With that arms akimbo gesture. Gets them out of the house. Men get underfoot so. This, in Redes, in high summer is the best time of the day. No trippers yet. Charo washing down the terrace in front of her bar, O Pousada do Marinero, been doing that all her life.

A bit short on water. Two two-gallon cans. Not too heavy when full. Put those in the dinghy. With the rubbish. Lift the cabin sole. Open the connecting cock, allows the port hand water tank to drain across to the starboard.

When you have filled both. Close that cock again and you have a reserve. And the full can you keep back, wedged by the companionway steps. Replace the cabin sole. Charo will let you fill the cans from her lock up next to the bar. Careful, mind you, for she is not obliged to:

'You turn that tap ON. And that tap ON. And when the can is full you turn that tap OFF. And that tap OFF. And mind, not a drop spilled. Understand Martin?'—pause—

'Sure?' (With a doubtful look).

'Yes, Charo, promise.'

What is the tide doing? Not far to go to low water.

'Come on Luis, we need to get a move on.'

For at low water you cannot reach the foot of the slipway. Which means manhandling the dinghy barefoot. *Pingos* (thornback rays) lurking. Quick check on the provisions. Ashore for a bath. Luis likes his newspaper. *La Voz de Galicia*, and so do I. But not for the same reason. How, you wonder is the saga of the errant one horned goat going? Or *Blanquita* the cow?

Scan the pages hopefully and there it is:

> Another heroic chapter in the annals of the Protección Civil, but this time they had to rescue a cow of 150 kilos weight which had fallen down a precipice 70 metres in height in the Río Landro, in Muras. 'Blanquita' came to rest on a small ledge, thus escaping sure death. The officials of the Presidencia of the Environment coordinated the operation. But it was four battle-hardened young lads from the Protección Civil of Cervo who rigged the lines, descended the precipice, manoeuvred the animal onto a stretcher and secured the feet with a harness. And hoisted the beast, aided by fourteen people pulling from above and the animal itself which did not move a muscle. Three hours of work brought the operation to a successful conclusion and all were happy [and, surely adjourned to the nearest bar]. Neighbours and the Garderia Forestal also lent a hand [ages since there had been so much excitement]. 'True artists and professionals' commented the delegado de Medio Ambiente.

Talk about hyperbole. But *La Voz* knows exactly what their readers want. And me too. Their daily dose of *Galicia profunda*, without the trouble of going there.

Later, maybe, we will sail.

As the morning wears on, so the heat increases. The little southerly has died. This is high pressure weather and the winds are predictable. Dawn will bring glassy calm. And fishing. Then for a while that southerly. Which dies. A wait, a baking hot, wipe the brow, seek the shade, wait. And then, early afternoon, the first hint. The water ruffles. The boat swings obedient to the new wind. And it drops, only to start again. A sharper gust. A foretaste. For come late afternoon the wind will be whistling down from the bluffs, whitecaps up to windward, blackened water as the next squall comes, enough to have you luffing a touch, spill the wind until it eases.

And if, as happens sometimes, there is a bit more east in the wind than normal. Then in the supposedly sheltered bay that is the head of the *ría*, the squalls are quite something, such is the effect of the hills. Gentle afternoon sail? Forget it.

16

'A Bit of a Chancer'

In his own words, that. But an engaging chancer, is Ian.

As to what he is doing in these pages, there can only be one reason. Sailing. But not sailing as you or I might imagine, or the modern world demands, all neat and tidy, chart plotters, crew, courses, blogs, God help us, wittering away about this and that, as if anyone was interested.

No. Ian had never sailed. His boat was, well it floated, to begin with anyway. He had no crew. And he decided to cross the Bay of Biscay bound, his constant refrain, for Gibraltar. Learning to sail on the way.

Tut. Well perhaps, but he is in honourable company. For he is not the first, nor will he be the last, to set out in a tangle of optimism and accidents to arrive, was it ten days or two weeks later, on the north coast of Spain. Where, for several years he remained. Dreaming his dream.

On the proverbial shoestring.

Of which you can disapprove or try to help.

Oh, and tut again, he drinks rather too much.

But he was not to be defeated. Though the boat, as round and tubby as a duck in a pond, languished rather, blistering heat, strip plank construction and a concrete hard not being a recipe for staunchness. In short, she leaked, whenever launched, like a sieve, to be hauled out again for another coat of bitumen or whatever he could lay his hands on.

The engine failed. Was repaired after a fashion and failed again. And became so much unwanted ballast. The dinghy disappeared. Stolen spluttered

Ian. Perhaps. Perhaps not. Life-raft? No.

But at the masthead, a cheeky little dog as a wind vane. Which was somehow apt.

And then one day he was gone.

Until a call came.

'Where are you Ian?'

'In Malpica.'

Which is on the *Costa de la Muerte*. With which you do not flirt. They towed her in, damaging her in the process, yanked her out, deposited her on the town quay and demanded salvage. It was the end.

'Come and strip her. Plenty of useful gear.'

And so there was.

Ian could write a book about it, entitled perhaps *Desperate Voyage*. (Sounds familiar? John Caldwell—the cutter *Pagan*). But he never will. So, this little cameo will have to do.

The Crystal City (and the perils of politics)

Naval architects adopted the design of the windowed stern of a warship and applied them as balconies to many places in northern Spain including Galicia.

Hence *The Crystal City*.
    Which, as an explanation, is pure fantasy. But a nice idea.

And it is to the Crystal City we are bound, for it does not do to turn down an invitation from such an exalted a being as The Commodore of the *Real Club Naútico de A Coruña*, so we did not. It was tall ships time and they wanted classics to make up the numbers. A boisterous sail and a good deal of wriggling found us in the inner basin, the *darsena*, for the duration, in Pete's case to enjoy the fleshpots of a city and in mine to revisit old haunts.

For it was here that I first made the acquaintance of Spain, initially on a swinging mooring, then ashore at the yacht club, and when that paled, which was quickly, in a dive by the name of TBO. An illegal night bar and a very good place to come to grips with the language and to begin to understand what makes the place tick.

But you have somehow to take the first step. You have no Spanish to talk of. You have no friends here. There appear to be no English people in the City. (This is not the *costas*, but rain-swept Galicia). So you explore. Find a likely looking place, a 'tea room' as it happened, serving rather more than tea, with all kinds of rather Arabic hangings, and a fey long-fingered lad drumming furiously at the bar with a rapt expression you hesitate to interrupt. The proprietor.

Wondering slightly what kind of reception to expect.

'*Hola*. I am an anarchist and my name is Luis'. Spoken in that order.

And with that, so to speak, you are in. For Luis (not crew Luis, but another) lost no time in taking his new-found friend to the illegal dive for a crash course in just about everything. 'Anarchist' here is not some quaint eccentricity, but a serious business, and Luis was the genuine article, albeit burnt out. A child of the post-Franco years, of the barricades, of strikes, of run-ins with the none too gentle *Guardia Civil*, he was one of many who bent the outsider's ear, night after night. Modern, democratic, prosperous Spain seemed very distant here. For all was memory, anger, disdain for the bourgeoisie and the conventional.

With a fair dose of *You have no idea what it was like,* (in post-Franco Spain, under the dictatorship, in the Civil War). All true enough, but an element of fanning the flames, or fighting old and long-lost battles, an odd kind of nostalgia. Curiously *rive gauche* in a way. And just as dated. And just as alluring.

Now, back to the water for a contemporary view of Spain under, since we are on the subject, marginally, the *dictadura*, courtesy Hugo Duplessis, *The perils of politics, Cruising Franco's Spain 1949,* which, with his (now I am sorry to say posthumous) permission is reproduced here. He is caught up in a visit by the 'Great Man' to Corunna, and this is what he has to say:

> We found the town [Corunna] busy preparing for the arrival of the great man himself, General Franco, El Caudillo, on his way to his holiday home in the cool Cordillera.
>
> Not for him the mere motor cavalcade, and what dignity is there in a helicopter, even if Spain had such a machine. No, he would arrive by sea, and in no ordinary ship, but the flagship of the Spanish Navy, the cruiser Miguel de Cervantes, followed like ducklings by the rest of his Navy.
>
> The local Club Naútico politely warned us that it would be wiser for us to move out into the harbour as we would be in the way and might get dam-

aged. It was soon clear why. All morning the long, wide quay filled up with company after company of soldiers in blue grey uniforms. It looked as if half the army was needed to greet the great leader. The uniforms and helmets had a strong resemblance to the German army of unhappy recent memory. The marching troops were goose stepping too. Yet this was 1949. Four years after VE day. Had we really won the war? Were they rising up to fight again in this far corner of Spain? Franco had wisely kept Spain out of our war, but it was well known where his sympathies lay.

It was before the days of compulsory courtesy flags and fussy police fining or even imprisoning offenders. As a consequence, I had never bothered, but now I could see that the few other foreign flag vessels were all flying them. Perhaps we should too. Our quandary was that Britain and the other victorious democracies had broken off diplomatic relations with fascist Spain. Should one fly as a courtesy the flag of a country with which one's own country was in some sort of discourtesy? Naively thinking the world was now at peace, I had never bothered to ask whether or not we should have gone to Spain at all. As a student engineer, the niceties of diplomacy were not my subject. What did it all mean? I had no reason to be discourteous. Quite the opposite. Our initial reception was now just a funny story. It would only be polite. Upholding the honour of the RCC.

Then came the next problem: where do we find a Spanish flag? All the shops were now behind this military tattoo. We asked the Club if we could borrow one, but all their flags were in use, draped along the balconies, even their table cloths, as they 'Dressed Ship'. Back on board we looked for any rags or fancy dish clothes that could be cobbled together to look something like a courtesy flag. Then at last the club boatman came out with a big faded bundle he had found hidden at the back of his boat store. It was a flag all right—a huge Spanish flag, as big as a blanket. The spreaders bent as Peter hoisted it amid much cheering and clapping and obvious approval from nearby boats.

He looked at it critically. 'Have you noticed, there is a sort of faded patch in the middle?'

'Probably some emblem. They used to have a king.'

'Those holes where the sun is shining through. They look too even and round for moths.'

'Bullets?'

'The right size.'

'I suppose you're going to suggest those brown stains are blood,' I laughed.

'Well. What do you think?'

'Oh dear. Some of those who cheered us did seem a bit overenthusiastic.'

'Clenched fists too.'

'Damn all we can do about it. Stuck here in the middle. A hundred thousand men on the shore. A hundred thousand guns. All pointing our way. Artillery too.'

'Yes, we are a bit out-numbered.'

'Nothing for it. We'll just have to say our prayers and hope it was the right side.'

Whether it was or not, we shall never know. We did not spark an international incident and nobody frog marched us off to face a firing squad because the problem solved itself. At the very moment when my light signal line broke under the extra weight, all eyes were on the cruiser, trying to identify which of those small blobs on the bridge was the man who was the reason for it all. So, nobody noticed when we really did insult the national flag (whichever it was) by letting it fall into the water.

By then we had spent several uncomfortable hours at anchor waiting with the other small craft. It was hot. Nothing seemed to be happening. There was some delay. Rumours. Troops were still arriving, each with its own band. As it got hotter, the rows of soldiers in their thick ceremonial uniforms were clearly uncomfortable. It should have been siesta. Gaps appeared in their ranks.

Then almost without warning the bows of the cruiser appeared from behind the old fortress on the point and made its way slowly across the harbour. The troops sprang to attention. The bands played the National Anthem, all together but each to its own time. Batteries fired a salute, which was answered by the ship. Every boat in the harbour blew its siren, as did the cars and buses. Crowds cheered, fireworks, and anything on shore that could make a noise joined in. Politics forgotten, we did too, Peter with a saucepan lid and me with the frying pan.

Because of the civil war and pre-war politics, Spain had been slow to modernise. We had noticed that most of the fishing boats and other small craft were steam powered. Consequently, as the ship docked and the noise at last died down, the harbour was littered with craft of all sizes and colours from trawlers and coasters to fishing boats and pleasure craft, all unable to move. They had literally run out of steam.

The old fortress on the point to which Hugo Duplessis refers is the Castel San Anton, overlooked in turn by the San Carlos gardens, for which *some corner of a foreign field that is forever England* could have been invented. Walled, shaded by centennial elms, nearly always deserted, the memorials here are nearly all British, starting with the tomb of Sir John Moore and that other poem, engraved in marble, passing on to the one shipwreck it would be intrusive to write about.

> Sacred to the memory of 172 officers and men of The Royal Navy who died at their post on board Her Britannic Majesty's Ship SERPENT wrecked on Boi rock near Cape Villano about 36 miles from this spot, on 10th November 1890. This stone was placed by the officers and men of HMS *Lapwing* in respectful remembrance. England expects every man to do his duty.

And ending with Wellington's address after the battle of San Marcial, the Peninsula Wars, eulogizing (in rather odd prose) the bravery of his Galician troops. *Spaniards, imitate the bravery of the inimitable Galicians.*

But there is something else. For here is the site of the final assault on the city by that notorious pirate and filibuster Sir Francis Drake. Well that is how he is seen here. He failed. Indeed to judge by English accounts did not really try that hard. But every siege, and it was a siege, needs a hero, or heroine. In this case Maria Pita. For it was the women of the town who put backbone into the defenders.

> Bringing up stones, earth, timber and other things [as to what 'other things' see below] as well as water, wine, food, so that the defenders should at no time abandon their post. And some of the said women arming themselves with pikes, on the day the general assault was ordered, the mines detonated, and the batteries opened fire, fought nobly, killing numbers of the enemy, hurling down missiles.

Chief among 'said women', Maria Pita. Heroine of the hour.

And who, if you ask me, was the world's original fishwife.

For when not busy killing off Elizabethan soldiers María Pita ('neither peaceable nor respectful' says our local historian, archly) got through no less than four husbands, was found guilty of attempted murder (and duly exiled but seems to have contrived to ignore it). And *armed with chamber pots full of three-week-old faeces and other filth* did her best, [with a rabble she had roused], to polish off the luckless soldier billeted in her home.

No wonder Drake retreated.

Presumably holding his nose.

Off to have a look at a shipwreck. Plenty of those here.

18

The Wreck of the 'Aegean Sea'

There is a lovely Spanish word, *rocambolesco*, which in fact derives from the French *rocambole* and means, roughly speaking, fantastic, exaggerated or extraordinary. And the players in this particular tragi-comic story are one Captain Konstadinos Stavidris, a Greek ship's master, promoted beyond his years, a touch over-confident; a harbour pilot, whose abilities arguably left something to be desired, and shadowy, in the background, the vision of two fat cats dining with brandy and cigars, masters of all they surveyed, whose baleful influence led to a disaster second only to the Prestige.

The prelude is a poster, so remarkable that I believed it a photomontage, until disabused. It shows that other emblem of Corunna, the Torre de Hercules, the 'Roman' lighthouse, honey coloured in the morning sunlight, against a background of inky black swirling clouds of burning oil.

The death throes of an oil tanker, the *Aegean Sea*.

The entrance to Corunna, to the uninitiated, appears a wide bay, innocent of dangers. The reality is different, for that wide innocent bay harbours a hidden reef Los Yacentes, over which in the frequent winter storms, the seas break with great violence. In short, not a nice spot at all. The Admiral, in his usual deadpan prose describes it thus:

> Local weather and sea state. 3.127. The inlet [he means Corunna] is open to W and NW winds and shelter can only be obtained in the port area on the W side. When a sea is running Banco Yacente is covered in breakers which, in

heavy NW gales, extend across the E channel to Punta del Seixo Blanco making this entrance impossible.

Impossible or not, that, the East channel is closed to the likes of the *Aegean Sea* on account of an earlier disaster, the *Urquiola*, another oil tanker, which impaled itself on an unknown (sort of) pinnacle rock, limped into port and was ordered out again, only to impale herself a second time on the same rock, on this occasion terminally so. A story just as *rocambolesco* as the one on which we are about to embark.

Corunna has an oil refinery, located to the west of the city, but the oil terminal is located within the city proper, connected to the refinery by a system of underground pipes, a cause for a certain nervousness for those of too vivid an imagination. Luis, for example, whose visions of apocalypse know no bounds. The refinery is a major employer and the slightest interruption of supplies is anathema to the powers that be. In this case those fat cats, musing over their brandy. Oblivious to all but profit. (A touch, but only a touch, polemical).

Now to the ship.

The ship was the *Aegean Sea*, a double hulled OBO (ore/bulk oil carrier) length 261.02 metres, beam 40.67 metres, drawing, fully laden 15.93 metres, 26,100 BHP, 114,000 tons DWT, single screw, 100 A-1 at Lloyds, loaded with 79,081 tons of Brent crude destined for the Repsol refinery in Corunna. Subsequent investigations showed that the ship had passed all the relevant inspections satisfactorily. Her crew of 28 were half Filipino, half Greek.

We are in the month of December 1992. The *Aegean Sea* had left Sullom Voe some days earlier with orders for Corunna, a port that Konstadinos Stavidris had never entered, never mind, as he was about to do so, at night, and in conditions when by rights the port should have been closed to a ship such as his.

The Admiralty pilot gives directions for entering the port by the West channel of too great a complexity to reproduce here, except to say that the thing is done on a very precise course $108\frac{1}{2}°$ (note the $\frac{1}{2}°$) passing between

Los Yacentes and the shore starting *from a position about 2 miles WNW of Punta Herminia (43°24' N, 8°24' W)*.

The two miles are significant. You need room. You are about to insert the proverbial needle, your lumbering great oil tanker, into a haystack, in the shape of a narrow channel, flanked by rocks and reefs, on leading marks, with a sharp turn to starboard at the bottom, by which time, you trust, the pilot will be aboard and tugs ready to assist.

He never got that far.

Instead, cooling his heels at anchor in the Ría de Ares, on a foul night, about to get a good deal fouler, he receives orders to enter port. It gives some idea of the conditions prevailing that it took a full hour to raise the anchor, and even then, only by steaming ahead. (The Ría de Ares is completely exposed to W through NW winds). Someone therefore gave the order to enter when palpably they should not have done. The pilot, in the full knowledge that his *jefe* was dining with the managing director of the oil refinery? Overruled perhaps from above? The master could have refused? But at what price? All is speculation, but it is not too difficult to guess.

The Ría de Ares lies to the east of Corunna. Which meant that to get his ship onto the leading marks of $108\frac{1}{2}°$, Captain Konstadinos Stavidris would have to steam several miles NNW (268° to be precise), until 2 miles WNW of Punta Herminia (the Roman lighthouse), when course would be altered to port, initially heading straight for the land, until clear of Los Yacentes and then fall off again onto those $108\frac{1}{2}°$ by which time, according to the rules, the pilot should have been aboard.

But it was too rough for the pilot to risk boarding at the normally appointed position, so he waited, some way down the channel, with a couple of tugs which he, the pilot had positioned on the leading marks to 'assist' the luckless, but slightly gung-ho Captain Konstadinos Stavidris, who (arguably) turned early, came onto 220°. And then to 190°. And there he stuck. For reasons not entirely clear, the *Aegean Sea*, in the midst of a violent squall and quite literally between a rock and a hard place, refused to respond to her helm. And with no sea room to stop, even supposing that was the intention, she ran

ashore at the foot of the Torre de Hercules.
> There to break her back and eventually go up in flames.
> They arrested the luckless Captain Konstadinos Stavidris.
> Who sensibly jumped bail.
> And was acquitted by the Greeks. Not so the Spanish.
> And he who gave the order?
> *Nunca máis*, they said. Never again.
> But then came the *Prestige*.

19

The Chiringuito in the Trees

'Just swing the lead will you, Luis.'
    'Three fathoms.'
'That will do. Let go.'
Bottom fine sand.

    Sometimes it is nice to have a gentle sail. None of that on your ear stuff, or scrabbling around in the dark, wondering just where on earth you might be. Or wriggling into an impossible gulch.
    No. Just a nice easy sail.
    You glide, almost majestically, under square sail and main, down the narrows in Ferrol, a commanding wind for once. No squalls, for once. Time to exchange greetings with the fishermen in their punts, jigging for squid, for once.
    For this is a holiday passage, unashamedly so. Ten miles across the head of the *ría*, in the July heat, bound for a settlement called Mera. Which is tucked in behind the point of the same name, where you have not been before, and where you propose to do nothing more exciting than spend an afternoon doing nothing in particular. And then, when the sun goes, ashore for a bite to eat and a glass or three.
    And there is the novelty. A new place. Round the headland, harden up on a summer breeze, and you open up a sheltered bay. An altogether gentler world, low headlands replace lofty capes, fields windswept heath. Over

your shoulder lies Corunna and ahead a wide sandy beach, towards which you tack, until that order *That will do. Let go.*

Clear water, that blessed wind, for it is fiendishly hot.

And you have reached, what can only be described as a kind of Spanish Butlins. A string of floating buoys protects the swimmers from that bane of all our lives, the jet ski. Tinkly music, balloons, buckets and spades. A scene straight out of the 1960s. And charming in its banality.

Sauntress and *Martlet*, a cable or so off, anchor chain visible in clear waters, and enticingly, on a bluff, amongst the pines, that most Spanish of institutions, the *chiringuito*, little more than a shack, and there, you hope, they will serve food. The bay is shallow. Far too shallow for merchant ships. And the water warm.

In winter here, not a soul. For in winter the great rollers sweep in from the west, rising ever higher as they reach the shoals, to fling themselves against the cliffs of Seixo Blanco in thunderous explosions of spume, hurrying clouds above. But in summer, on a day like this, should you venture ashore all is dust, heat, crowds, and endless stalls. A quick foray is quite enough. You retire to your ship, clutching milk, bread or whatever it was you needed.

The sun dips. The beach empties as though on a command. And peace descends. As for the vanished holidaymakers, they will all be tucking in happily somewhere, shrimping nets at the ready for tomorrow. That fortnight's holiday away from the daily grind.

(God, how patronising can you get? But the flavour, the flavour is there).

G and T Geraldine?

'What a nice idea Martin.'

'Aboard *Martlet*?'

Well yes, because they have ice.

Set the anchor light first. Row across. Scramble up the boarding ladder.

'Cheers.'

'Cheers Pete.'

Martlet, aboard which we have just stepped, is a yacht with pedigree. No 720 from Morgan Giles yard, she was built for the Britannia Royal Naval College of teak on oak, (the teak brought back from Burma by the Royal Navy says Pete, with a touch of nostalgia, when yachts were yachts and ships were ships, he being an engineer of the old school and all). She was built as a sail training vessel, 43ft long, 9ft beam, 6ft 10in draught. Originally without auxiliary power and with fractional rig. Launched 1959 and still going strong. One of five identical yachts built for the Royal Navy by Morgan Giles. And how that yard must have hummed. Five ships in the build. No expense spared. And now just another housing estate.

'Do you think they will have food, Martin?'

Only one way to find out. Ashore in the inflatable, rubbish in hand, looking for a bin. Carry the inflatable up the beach. Above the high-water line. Up the steps and onto a veranda. Open to the skies. Dusk has reached the velvet stage. Lights begin to twinkle. To the accompaniment of that most evocative of sounds, cicadas, the music of heat and stillness and herb scented, sweet night air, that all too heady mix.

We are on holiday, remember. The food is all we could wish for. The wine flows. The place is neither empty (which would be dreary). Nor full, which would be tiresome.

'Where are you from?'

'The yachts down there.'

Which you are admiring in that proprietorial kind of way. And it strikes you. This is like a railway poster of the Côte d'Azur. In whatever period it was when the *train bleu* still ran, and all yachts were white, made of wood, and elegant in their lines.

No other craft.

Stars twinkle. The riding light a pinprick.

One of those moments.

'Know how many topsails there are on this coast Pete?'

'No.'

'Three.'

'When we first came there was just one. Us.'

Then *El Portugués* conceded the point and there were two. In the same *ría*, the same anchorage. And now *Eltoraji*, up in Ribadeo.

Makes a difference, a topsail, no doubt about it. Not easy to set properly, but once set (and on a calm day, set all on the mooring, row off and cast a critical eye. Halyard a wee bit higher on the pole? Main peaked up a fraction more?) the icing on the cake. And there is a little trick. Put two reefs in the mainsail and still you can set that topsail. Halyard to the top of the pole now, sheet and downhaul as before, but add a leader to the heel of the pole and bring it snug to the mast.

Why bother?

Pride in your ship. I mean she looks good. All of a piece. And goes like the proverbial.

20

The Great Mushroom Hunt

'Tomorrow morning at 7 o'clock. All right? And wrap up well.'
'O.K. Regino. We will be there.'
'And bring a *cesta*,' (wicker basket).
The great mushroom hunt, courtesy Regino.

We wend our way up and up, bound for *Galicia profunda* (deep rural Galicia), a phrase pregnant with meaning. For you do not mess with *Galicia profunda*, nor with its inhabitants, *los campesinos*, notoriously jealous of their rights, suspicious of outsiders, clinging to ancient beliefs, and prone to softness in the head (a tad too much inbreeding).

Pass a roadside bar, brightly lit, There, they are. Knocking back *aguardiente* and strong coffee, the *campesinos*, hunting dogs and a muddy 4 x 4.

'They are after *jabalí*.'

So, it would appear we are to share the woodlands of *Galicia profunda* not only with mushrooms, but wild boar and gun toting slightly inebriated *campesinos*.

'Don't worry Martin, I have these,' producing a fistful of firecrackers, 'I let them off, so they know we are not wild boar.'

Very reassuring, I am sure.

Were it not for remembering a particular episode, involving Luis, eggshells and *Galicia profunda*, an innocent enough mix you might think. Wrong. He is packing up his tent, burying every last trace of his presence, including egg shells. What happens? Over the horizon erupts, enraged, a *campesino*, a son of the soil, wielding a sickle *'Vou te matar! Vou te matar!'* ('I will kill you! I will kill you!'). And whilst his mates might be killing themselves with laughter, Luis was running for his life. And why?

Because, bury an egg in a fallow field and no crop will grow, ever, again.

Surely you knew that?

We return relatively unscathed, physically speaking, with a basket filled with *níscalos, lenguas de vaca*, and other such delights.

And nerves in tatters.

Regino spends his holidays in Serbia. Wolves, bears and a good deal of heavy drinking. Which makes him an interesting person to know. In fact, the imagination runs riot. Serbia, for heaven's sake. The Balkans. Always trouble in the Balkans, however hazy one's geography. Aren't we in Transylvania or vampire land? The place which kept the lights burning in the European chancelleries at night.

Sarajevo.

And yet, and yet, that is where he goes on holiday.

Which probably says more about the writer than him.

For why not?

I have seen the photographs. That old fashioned welcome. The toasts. The hunt on the mountains. *Caza mayor* they call it here, going for the *jabalí*, or deer. And in the Balkans, rather more besides. Bears, I wouldn't wonder.

And he speaks the lingo.

Better than Benidorm. Is it not?

21

The Romance of a Proper Dinghy

> The light north-easterly breeze continued during my watch until midnight, and Juanita sailed on through the darkness, her jib shimmering with the phosphorescence of the lee bow wave, and little Punch, the 8' dinghy following in our glistening wake, with a ghostly light parting at his stem.
>
> *The Magic of the Swatchways. Maurice Griffiths.*

Chuckling, he might have written.

Or playful.

There is something about a clinker dinghy. Perhaps it is the *Swallows and Amazons* we all have in us. Childhood memories. Our first boat. Our first *sailing* boat. Catching a crab. Sculling.

So simple somehow.

How long did she take to build? Never mind. There comes, at last, the day of the launch. Open the front door, and out on her side, she goes. Varnish gleaming in the sunlight. Down to the slip. Looking perhaps a little too perfect. But time will see to that. The colours will soften. The bumps and scrapes. Inevitable. Scars of war. To be healed with paint and varnish.

The sweeps are long. Too long, complains Luis. But long sweeps mean long strokes, long deliberate strokes, and yes, she chuckles. Entranced, you take her on her first outing. A picnic on the beach round the headland. You could walk of course, but that is not the point. Load aboard the wicker hamper, a rug, the fishing gear, the bailer, and put your back into it. Not too much, nor do you need to, for she carries her way.

Steal up on *Martlet*. Take them by surprise.

'Come aboard.'

Because yes, it is Ribeiro time.

She lies docile, astern.

And she becomes, in a sense, everybody's property. 'May I...'

Yes of course you may. For she is not only fun. She is practical. A load carrier. Safe in a chop. Big party to get aboard. Use the dinghy. Luis morning fishing. Stand in the dinghy. Need to bring a spar ashore. Use the dinghy.

Off to Ferrol. Tow the dinghy. Because there is that anchorage. And ashore, in Mugardos, *pulpo*, again. But keeps him quiet does a plate of *pulpo*. A wooden platter. Olive oil. A sprinkling of *pimentón*, bread to mop up the last of the olive oil. And that is lunch.

Later we will add a rig. But not yet.

We acquire, from where, I cannot remember, a pair of coir fenders. Which look the part. Indeed, are the part. For unlike plastic they do not squeak when the dinghy is alongside. And whilst *Sauntress* cannot speak (but of course she does, all the time, for each and every sound is familiar, tap, tap, tap, 'you have forgotten to frap the halyards', grating sound on the bobstay, 'you have forgotten to loop the chain over the fairlead'), she is happy. Dinghy alongside, she preens herself. Look at us, she says.

Aren't we just a picture?

And yes. They are.

It also got something out of the system. A yen to build a boat. To restore, or properly, to refit, a boat is one thing. To build a boat, from scratch, another. Month after month she lay, wrong side up, at the bottom of the stairs, reproving. 'When are you going to steam the next plank?' 'Soon, promise.' For you remember the garboard strake. The first strake to fit and by far the most difficult. Twice you made it. Twice you split it. And once split, then for all the work, you must start again. As we did.

You turn her over at last. Start on the ribs at last. And then one day, bless me. We have finished.

And to have an 8' clinker dinghy as tender to your yacht puts you immediately in a different class. Up there with the smacks, the Bawleys and the Thames Barges. Joining the aristocracy. A working aristocracy admittedly and all the better for that. So, Pete built a dinghy as well. Same design. Same reason. And same, for I know it, that same sense of pride. As in doing something worthwhile. Which with luck will outlive you.

She has all the accoutrements. Anchor, bailer, sponge, rings in the stem and stern-post, painter forward, painter aft, lash the sweeps to the thwarts, and when towing her, a trick. Where it came from I don't know. But the voice said, watch it in a following sea. Because your docile little dinghy will convert in a flash into a fiend. Roaring down the face of a wave to brain herself on the counter. Ah yes. Secure a warp to the aft ring and bring that aboard on the counter. With that you can tame her.

Except…….

You forget to secure that warp on the transom, a light lashing would have done it. You are reaching for home, sheets started, lee rail under, the dinghy, nose in air, astern. Feeling smug. In an instant the yacht goes from alive to dead. Glance astern and there is the reason. The warp has slipped over.

And you are damn nearly stopped.

So that is what is meant by trailing warps, that *Heavy Weather Sailing* technique. Amazing. We cannot get it in. Both trying.

Another lesson learned.

You row home under a gibbous moon.
Softly, on dark waters.
Dreaming.

22

La Costa de la Muerte

> *... One of the most terrible, rocky, and dangerous coasts that a ship could possibly encounter... so inhospitable is the shore that no vessel, however big, or however well built, could live for five minutes if driven on to the land, which is much more rocky even than that in the neighbourhood of Land's End.'*
>
> The Times. *November 1890.*

The mariner's nightmare. The *Costa de la Muerte* runs from Corunna in the east to Cape Finisterre in the west. The frequency of shipwrecks is matched only by the outpourings of every literary pen that has passed, fascinated, and horrified by turns, by what they witnessed.

> It was not without reason that the Latins gave the name of Finis terrae to this district. We had arrived exactly at such a place as in my boyhood I had pictured to myself as the termination of the world, beyond which there was a wild sea, or abyss, or chaos. I now saw far before me an immense ocean, and below me a long and irregular line of lofty and precipitous coast. As for myself, when I viewed that wide ocean and its savage shore, I cried, 'Such is the grave, and such are its terrific sides; those moors and wilds, over which I have passed, are the rough and dreary journey of life. Cheered with hope, we struggle along through all the difficulties of moor, bog, and mountain, to

arrive at what? The grave and its dreary sides Oh, may hope not desert us in the last hour hope in the Redeemer and in God!

George Borrow. The Bible in Spain

The reason for this reputation was, and to some extent still is, this. Cape Finisterre and the *Costa de la Muerte* lie on the track of any vessel bound south from the English Channel to the Mediterranean or beyond. And conversely northbound. The former after a long Biscay crossing, often in thick weather, when, in the days before radar, radio direction finders and GPS, the master if unable to fix his position by sextant sight, the sky being overcast, was left with dead reckoning, an imprecise science at the best of times. Compounded by unpredictable currents setting into the bay, magnetic anomalies, and leeway. This meant that until he sighted land, assuming he did, the master would be none too sure of his vessel's whereabouts. The one salvation being to take soundings, which would warn the mariner of the proximity of the land. Which HMS *Serpent*, for example, signally failed to do.

As to what awaited the shipwrecked mariner ashore, the more inventive pens waxed eloquent. Here for example is *The Times*, 'the thunderer' in 1924. Which is worth quoting in full, if rather for the apocalyptic prose than the content:

> In the last months of winter and during early spring the iron-bound coastline of Galicia between the Minho's mouth and Finisterre is lashed with westerly gales, which batter the bastions of its granite cliffs with hurricane salvos of their tremendous artillery. Such storms intimidate the most imperturbable of 'extranjeros', but not the saturnine Gallego fisherfolk, who, like the Cornishmen and Western Scottish Highlanders during the last century, are wreckers and beach-brigands to a man, and welcome the fury of the Atlantic for the harvest which it may bring them.
>
> A dour, hard-visaged race, austere, methodical, and avaricious, the Gallegos –like their savage Suevian ancestry– are harsh as the rocky headlands on their coasts. Their fishing is done by grey-haired men and boys, for, as

a Galician youth approaches man's state, he goes at once to other parts of Spain and Portugal, or else to South America, to tempt fortune as a labourer or domestic servant. In Madrid, in Lisbon, and in Buenos Aires you find him in his hundreds, tough, dependable, industrious. But, as the years creep on, nostalgia will surely take him home again, where all the time his womenfolk have been ploughing and reaping, driving his team, and helping his father with the fishing-nets. Gloomy and superstitious as the Hebridean Celts, their wreck-strewn shores are peopled for them by supernatural figures and haunted with dark and sinister traditions.

The Times then adds, for good measure, this little gem.

THE LADY OF THE ROCKS
A Galician legend. From a correspondent

Remarkable among these legends is that of the Lady of the Rocks (La Señorita de las Rocas), the apparition of a pale and beautiful woman, indistinguishable almost from the wraithlike spray-mists, which is said to appear during storms of exceptional fury and is a presage of imminent evil.

Long years ago, they say, one stormy night in March –una tempestad terrible! - an English barque was driven ashore not far from Cape Fernandez, and all the folk thereabout flocked beachwards, hoping for what the wind and waves might send them. They watched the unhappy vessel shattered on a reef of rocks some 200 yards from the cliffs, and the surface of the intervening water was soon covered by tossing wreckage and despairing swimmers.

But, as they looked, the spars and barrels and piteous writhing bodies sank before their eyes, and then occurred a marvel. Upon a protuberant slab of rock, well within wading distance, the surf washed up the drooping form of a fair young girl of wondrous beauty, veiled all in white, wringing her hands and weeping bitterly; her pale gold hair and pearly clinging garments unnaturally effulgent against the surrounding blackness of the storm. The women of Galicia are thickset and swarthy, and doubtless this frail blonde creature of the North, cast at their feet so unexpectedly, seemed to them something from another world. Nor could they credit that, if indeed human, she could have won to shore when so many powerful swimmers had failed. This could be no mortal, but a sprite or witch in league with Satanás. 'Stone her!' the women howled in their gruff Gallego dialect, calling upon their patron Saint Iago, whose bones –once miraculously preserved from the infidel Almanzor– lay but a few score miles away at Compostela. A shower of stones hurtled seaward and battered what was left of her life out of the body of the unfortunate girl, and, in a revulsion of horror, the murderers fled without waiting for their prospective harvest.

Ever afterwards during the westerly storms of Spring it is whispered that one may see the white figure from the sea, eerily waving its arms above the faint glory of its dripping hair; and if one does, 'Dios, eso es un infortunio!' and one should make one's peace with God and settle one's affairs without delay.

Which libellous passage might well give the spinster, with her cup of tea by the fireside, a suitable frisson of horror, but contrasts sharply with this comment from a survivor of the wreck of the *Great Liverpool*, 24th February 1846.

…the extreme kindness and hospitality of the Spaniards towards us; they did all in their power to relieve our wants even supplying us with clothes gratis…

Lines which ring so obviously true.

The lighter side of the *Costa de la Muerte* would go something like this, bearing in mind that constant refrain, Galicia is like Ireland. Which being the case, how about a spot of pillage, courtesy *Some Experiences of an Irish RM.*, Somerville and Ross. 1858:

For three days of November a white fog stood motionless over the country. All day and all night smothered booms and bangs away to the south-west told that the Fastnet gun was hard at work, and the sirens of the American liners uplifted their monstrous female voices as they felt their way along the coast of Cork. On the third afternoon the wind began to whine about the windows of Shreelane, and the barometer fell like a stone. At 11 P.M. the storm rushed upon us with the roar and the suddenness of a train; the chimneys bellowed, the tall old house quivered, and the yelling wind drove against it, as a man puts his shoulder against a door to burst it in.

The ship was, or had been, a three-masted barque; two of her masts were gone, and her bows stood high out of water on the reef that forms one of the shark-like jaws of the bay. The long strand was crowded with black groups of people, from the bank of heavy shingle that had been hurled over on to the road, down to the slope where the waves pitched themselves and climbed and fought and tore the gravel back with them, as though they had dug their fingers in. The people were nearly all men, dressed solemnly and hideously in their Sunday clothes; most of them had come straight from Mass without any dinner, true to that Irish instinct that places its fun before its food. That the wreck was regarded as a spree of the largest kind was sufficiently obvious. Our car pulled up at a public-house that stood askew between the road and the shingle; it was humming with those whom Irish publicans are pleased to call 'Bona feeds,' and sundry of the same class were clustered round the door. Under the wall on the lee-side was seated a bagpiper, droning out 'The Irish Washerwoman' with nodding head and tapping heel, and a young man was cutting a few steps of a jig for the delectation of a group of girls.

So far Murray's constabulary had done nothing but exhibit their imposing chest measurement and spotless uniforms to the Atlantic, and Bosanquet's coastguards had only salvaged some spars, the debris of a boat, and a dead sheep, but their time was coming. As we stumbled down over the shingle, battered by the wind, and pelted by clots of foam, someone beside me shouted, 'She's gone!' A hill of water had smothered the wreck, and when it fell from her again nothing was left but the bows, with the bowsprit hanging from them in a tangle of rigging. The clouds, bronzed by an unseen sunset, hung low over her; in that greedy pack of waves, with the remorseless rocks above and below her, she seemed the most lonely and tormented of creatures.

About half-an-hour afterwards the cargo began to come ashore on the top of the rising tide. Barrels were plunging and diving in the trough of the waves, like a school of porpoises; they were pitched up the beach in waist-deep rushes of foam; they rolled down again and were swung up and shouldered by the next wave, playing a kind of Tom Tiddler's ground with the coastguards. Some of the barrels were big and dangerous, some were small and nimble like young pigs, and the bluejackets were up to their middles as their prey dodged and ducked, and the police lined out along the beach to keep back the people. Ten men of the R.I.C. can do a great deal, but they cannot be in more than twenty or thirty places at the same instant; therefore, they could hardly cope with a scattered and extremely active mob of four or five hundred, many of whom had taken advantage of their privileges as 'bona-fide travellers,' and all of whom were determined on getting at the rum.

Which seems a good deal closer to the truth. For that could just as well be Galicia today. The grip of the law is at best tenuous, and at times conspiratorial. Should a container ship lose a few? An entire village with identical yellow shoes. Or carton upon carton of cigarettes. And one for the *Guardia Civil*. Or printers. Lots of printers. Though it is hard to see what the women of Camariñas, busy lacemaking, will do with those. Or condensed milk. But here we are on dangerous territory. For the label is in German, or Chinese, or Arabic. Looks like paint. Goes on like paint. All the houses white. All very pretty.

Until the flies come.

One November day. All was uncharacteristically still. The sea like a polished mirror, reflecting the setting sun. We putter out on a fishing expedition, for we have been offered a short break, fisherman's house on the quay. Our host at the wheel. He is heading for a shoal patch. And joy of joys, he does not use a GPS. He uses transits.

Those small things which tell you that you are in capable hands. And bless me, the novice catches the one and only fish of the day.

Off, next day on the obligatory pilgrimage. *El Cementerio de los Ingleses*. The English cemetery. HMS *Serpent*. Where every year a wreath is laid still.

Where ships of her Majesty's navy fire a salute. And where, if you walk down to the shore, you can absorb the sense of desolation. For it is a desolate place. No houses. No trees. Reefs running far out to sea. Boi Rock, where she struck. A grey unquiet sea. You shiver in the cold wind, collar turned up.

Drizzle.

And turn for the roaring log fires of that fisherman's cottage in Corme. The rest of the story you pass over in respectful silence. Better like that. And Galician winters being what they are, you make sure to lay in a good supply of firewood, oak mostly. For if not the damp will get you. And where you write, as now, surrounded by log books, pilots, all the material you plunder for memory. To slip back, effortlessly to halcyon days. Or not.

But you can understand the seduction of such places. Close the door, light the fire, listen to the howling wind, straight from the Atlantic, hear the rumble and thunder of the waves (thank God, we are not at sea tonight), the electricity goes again. Against which candles and oil lamps and hot water bottles. And an awful lot of blankets.

Hermit-like.

El alemán de Camelle they called him. And he was precisely that, a hermit. Adopted by the inhabitants of Camelle. 'Do you know what he is doing Martin? He is piping us out.' *El Irlandés de Redes*, that kind of adopted. He was before my time. But you can understand why. Just as you can understand what killed him. The wretched *Prestige* and the oil which defiled his paradise.

La Costa de la muerte.

As seductive as it is lethal.

23

No Engine?

There is nothing to compare with the contrast. The big city and the office are left behind, the traffic too, cross the Strood and if you turn right, West Mersea, but turn left, on the island now, and you are on your way to one of the remotest spots you could wish for. Open the gate, drive down as far as you can and switch off the car engine at last. Silence, blessed silence. Open skies and the sudden cry of a curlew, and how the sound travels here. Or a water rail. Who knows? What counts is that it is a familiar and much-loved sound.

And if it is night, as usually it is, wait for your night vision. For there is nothing here. Brightlingsea away to your right, across the Colne, the lurid orange of street lights, but too far away to intrude.

Clamber the embankment, and there, dimly, is the dinghy, oars beneath, and out on the mooring another vague shape, waiting whitely, on dark waters, *Sauntress*. You have brought a stew, and provisions for the weekend. If the tide is out you have a long haul down to the water's edge, but I like it more at low tide. Your world, your cocoon, is smaller, more comforting almost. The mud uncovered, the banks so high you can see nothing beyond, the little sounds, the trickle of the tide, the popping of the mud. And another sudden plaintiff cry. Or, distantly the hoot of an owl.

In an hour or so the charcoal stove is glowing, the stew bubbling, the oil lamp lit. Later, you can listen to the wireless, another old friend, especially on Friday night, but for now, in the cockpit, in the stillness, glass in hand, you have a whole weekend to look forward to. Tomorrow, ashore perhaps for a pick your own, and maybe half a dozen oysters from the Kerrisons, the Colchester Oyster fishery, and, perhaps a regatta somewhere, or off to some anchorage, Osea Island being a favourite.

And it is in that haze of romance that the notion forms. What if no engine? Pretend it is not there. It keeps niggling this notion. Until one day you give the idea a trial. Today you are not going to use the engine. You know, in your heart of hearts you are cheating. For to drop the mooring under sail is hardly all that difficult, to anchor at Osea you have done dozens of times and to pick up the mooring again, under sail, that too you have done often enough.

Still, if you do not do it now, you never will.

So out it came.

Meanwhile, and many years earlier, something of the kind was going on. You could describe it as the other side of the engineless coin, the need to learn to handle your boat as they did of old; in a sense you could call it deliberately making life difficult for yourself.

And so it is. But therein lies the satisfaction.

Below, an extract from *Half a Gale*, by Michael Frost, published by Kenneth Mason 1981. *35 years' enchantment with an East Coast fishing smack*, called *Boadicea*. Which he worked as a smack should be worked, albeit he was not strictly a smacksman. Working the waters I know well, the Colne, the Blackwater, the Dengie flats, with St Peter on the Wall, that ancient Anglo/Celtic chapel all alone on the flatlands, so diminutive, yet so evocative, especially when bound through the Ray Sand, and more. In this case, the upper reaches of the Colne, where *Boadicea* lies on a mooring off Wivenhoe, which at low tide is little more than a ditch. Very much the last days of trawling under sail, date not given, but to judge by the reference to J class veterans, no later than the early 1950's. And Hervey, in the story which follows, of the old school, taciturn, solid, and a seaman to his fingertips. As he is about to show us.

> Hervey's new mast was ready to go to Wivenhoe and we arranged the ferry trip. We had already agreed that I should be skipper on the way round but

coming home he would be in charge and he now decreed that the smack would leave Wivenhoe half an hour before dead low water. It was about time I was taught how to turn a smack round. ... Here at low water the dredged channel was not much more than two smack's lengths across and raggingly I commented that in the morning I should be expecting something suitably impressive. Hervey brushed that aside. On a well run vessel the mate had no time to lounge around and criticise. I was to be on board at nine o'clock sharp and he would keep me out of mischief.

Next morning the wind was fresh south-westerly and when I crested the sea wall the smack was already under canvas ..., he had set up the hoist of the two-reefed main high-footed and with the gaff raised only to the horizontal. Close hauled on the port tack the smack was holding a sheer evenly balanced between wind and tide and I saw that he had given her the full scope of the mooring on the jib sheet bollard ... The channel looked perilously narrow, but my attention was mostly taken with the smack herself. She looked a picture of formal rectitude and I could sympathise with those who sometimes accused me of being blatantly ostentatious.

After launching my boat I began sculling off and now Hervey, appearing on deck, stood for a few moments looking aloft at the wind on the streamer. As I crossed the smack's bows he passed the time of day briefly, and as though to discourage further conversation moved to the foredeck and began setting up the staysail. When the sail was half way up the stay he stretched across to flick the mooring free and the vessel was already under way as I came alongside.

While I let the boat go aft he finished with the staysail and then cast off the fall of the peak. Holding the weight he paused to glance forward beneath the staysail as the smack began paying off at first slowly and then more quickly. Just before she was broadside to the wind he began hauling hand over fist at full stretch. Meantime the tiller was swinging free and for a moment I was tempted to take it and let the smack pick up way, but then thought better of it. If Hervey was working to a plan let him get on with it.

So far the smack was still idle in the water but where before she had been paying off she now steadied as she felt the peak and began slowly to draw ahead. Belaying the peak he carried straight on to free the staysail and then holding the weight paused again to watch the smack. As she gathered way she began to luff and at that moment had had the staysail down. I began to realise what he had in mind. His only chance of getting around in the width of water would be to use something along the lines of the backing and filling method of the trading brigs. I had never seen it done and had only hazy ideas about its operation, but vaguely I knew that when a vessel has to make a long and short leg beat in narrow waters, she cannot sail the short tack in the ordinary way without putting herself ashore. To avoid that she sails the short tack hove to, and then, being without steerage way, she can only make the second wending, by having her sails trimmed to swing her round. I had not heard of the method being used with fore and aft rig but clearly Hervey meant to try it. With luck he might just get away with it, but I would have taken a bet that the men watching from Wivenhoe Quay, J class veterans in Sunday morning rig, had already decided he hadn't a hope. The Colne is a bit public for taking win-or-lose chances.

Meanwhile *Boadicea* was fore-reaching slowly and at the same time she was turning. Without hurry he cast off all but the last turn of the peak halyard and then waited. The luff of the mainsail spilled its wind, but the leech was still drawing, and the smack was still turning. A moment later, as the boom swung inboard he cast off the fall and let the peak run fully down. He carried straight on to set up the foresail and then bowsed it flat on the starboard bowline. The smack was now in the wind's eye with her staysail a'back and she was still afloat. The first part of the turn had been carried through successfully but any moment now she would fall away like a ton of bricks and getting her back on course after that would be nigh on impossible.

The tiller which had been to starboard during the luff had now come idly amidships but then as the smack started to go astern it swung over hard a'port. The reverse helm tipped the balance and the smack began paying off. Harvey had the staysail down at once, and then to my surprise ignored the peak which I would have set up again as a matter of urgency. Instead, with a gesture of mock despair, he came aft to pick up a sweep with which he gave the smack two or three helping strokes over the quarter and still idle in the water she answered easily. When she was broadside to the wind, he laid the sweep aside and put one leg against the tiller to hold it hard down. I realised that his logic had been better than mine. With the peak down the smack had picked up way only slowly and this had given him much more time to get her round.

With the skipper at the helm my place was on the foredeck, so I moved forward to cast free the peak ready to set it up, but he seemed to be in no hurry and as the smack gathered way he jerked his thumb at a raised scar of mud showing close to leeward and shouted to me cheerfully that the dredged channel was as steep to as the side of a house. He nodded for the peak and I began hauling. Afterward I set up the staysail and when the falls were stowed, I went aft to join him.

And with that, they were away.
Chapeau, Hervey.

24

Blind Man's Buff

'That's a nice ship, Pete.'
Poking around on the pontoons, as one does, looking for something interesting.

'Looks like a Colin Archer type.'

'Could be. Very solidly built.'

We soon found out. For she was moved to lie alongside *Sauntress* and *Martlet*. A show within a show. And now yacht *Larry*, built 1907 by Camper and Nicholson, length overall forty-four feet. Owners that model of quiet unassuming competence which is the hallmark of a true seaman. And head and shoulders above the rest.

Our paths were to cross again.

Sounds like wind (in half sleep). But it was not. The tall ships were gone. In their place a monstrous cruise ship, the general commotion of which I had mistaken for wind. Fog had descended. And suddenly we felt trapped in this grey and forbidding place, tired of being imprisoned in granite walls, which is about all you see in the *darsena*. That and a plethora of that species which inhabit so many marinas, yachts that never put to sea.

'What do you think, Pete?'

'Perhaps it will clear.'

Perhaps it will. There is no wind.

We agree a tow for so long as needed. For a big passage lies ahead, up the coast, some fifty or more miles, to a port called Cariño. The charts are unfolded, the courses marked off. We hook up to *Martlet* in the gloom, and off, optimistically, we set. Clear the head of the breakwater, just visible and an impetuous blast, a ship somewhere. A momentary frisson until the pilot boat appears, inbound.

So, he has sent that ship on her way.

She won't bother us.

Oily swell.

The putter, putter, putter of Pete's engine. Yes, the sun is trying to break through. You must concentrate. Don't let her sheer on the end of the tow. Where Pete goes, you follow. But where is that? Dig out the Garmin. Ah! So that is where we are. Pete is on chart-plotter and radar. Without which this passage would be nigh on impossible.

Course change (the compass tells you that). Clear of Cabo Prior. 5 miles off. Our regulation distance from the headlands on this coast. A breath comes. You set the foresail. This adds maybe ½ a knot and takes a little of the strain off the tow.

Pete looks back and gestures in that despairing way. But what are we to do? Plug on, and on, and on. A fix now and again (the Garmin). Plot the position now and again. Against eventualities.

'Cedeira abeam. Want to go in?'

'No, Pete. Let's get this over with.'

Putter, putter, putter. Clammy, chilly, dreary. There are hours more of this ahead.

No, not Cedeira this time, but you remember. July, it was. The first season on this coast. Something of the innocent abroad. Log peppered with comments on architecture: Redes, *tumble of houses,* Ares, *horrible new buildings* (true enough). So how was Cedeira?

20.30. Wind. W 5. Very exciting entrance.

Which it most certainly was.

Cedeira, a port of refuge, says the Admiral, is entered on a series of leading marks. *The East side of the approach,* he continues, *is precipitous and steep rising to an elevation of over 300 metres, ... and is bordered by rocks and islets extending 1 cable offshore ... Punta Chirlateira on the W side of the entrance is rugged with above-water rocks and rocks awash close off it ... the entrance is 6 cables wide.*

You must line up on the leading marks. Which, if you are to avoid the above water rocks and rocks awash on the W side, puts you uncomfortably close, for a vessel relying solely on sail power, to the precipitous E side, complete with *rocks and islets* where the seas rebound, the word in the log is 'lumpy' and the wind fickle as it lifts over the high land.

That killer combination, lumpy seas, no wind, the ship helpless. And rocks a biscuit's toss away. You need to watch your step on this coast. Remember another log entry. *Beware Seixo Blanco.* The same reason. We strayed too close, lost the wind, lost steerage way, and for a short time were pointing straight at the rocks.

Oh, the joys of engineless sailing.

But Pete has one. Putter, putter, putter. Still it goes on. The sun has given up trying. In the cocoon. Not even a catspaw now.

He hauls round SE. At last. Thank goodness for that.

We must be clear of Los Aguillones.

This is, for all the hyperbole, legend, and general Celtic mysticism, a rather remarkable place. Here, two seas meet, the Cantabrian and the Atlantic. The cape, Cabo Ortegal, is the highest in Europe. The rocks of Los Aguillones are 1,160 million years old, amphibolite, being they say, the most ancient rock form known, formed, it is said at the centre of the earth, and thrown up in some convulsion and to the mariners of Cariño, this place has the rather curious title of *kilómetro zero*, meaning where the two seas meet.

Pete turns, gives the thumbs up and of a sudden we are in the clear. To windward appear Los Aguillones, those remarkable jagged pinnacle rocks, rather menacing in appearance, black against a background of fog. And over the bow Cariño. A squall descends from the heights, startling after a long windless day. Heightening the general feeling that we are tiptoeing past Valhalla. Putter, putter, putter, the last mile or so. Pete casts us off and we carry our way to anchor off the beach, too tired to do anything much. The long, long day is over. The fog curls over the great cape, but is held back, for, say the fishermen, it has been clear here all day.

The log contains the cryptic entry, *Very odd town clock*. But then *kilómetro zero* is odd too.

Why put ourselves through all this?

Because on the morrow, by appointment we have a pilot, one Alvaro by name.

25

The Bar at Santa Marta de Ortigueira.

11.91. General Information. Santa Marta de Ortigueira (43º43' N 7º51 W) stands on the E shore of the ría de Santa Marta de Ortigueira, an extensive landlocked estuary. The harbour accessible to coasters, is approached by a narrow tortuous channel between tidal flats. The entrance is obstructed by a bar.

11.192. Limiting conditions. Controlling depth over bar. 1.5 metres. ... Breakers form on the bar in any swell from the north and entry is seldom practicable in winter.

Admiralty sailing directions. Biscay Pilot. NP22

Alvaro appears next morning, wreathed in smiles, but impatient. Much though I would love to sail there is nothing for it but to take up station astern of *Martlet*, for not only is there the bar to negotiate, but the narrow tortuous channel as well. The sailing can and will come later.

Pete and I have studied the books and all that there is to be found about this entrance. They all concur. The deepest water is next to the island on the west side. We embark John 'Skipper' whose background is like Pete's, commercial fishing in Cornwall. A good man to have aboard.

It is a lovely morning. Not a trace of swell. No wind to talk of. The lead line is ready. The kedge is on deck. And the inflatable astern. For should we touch, we will need all three, and prompt. But we are in the hands of a man with local knowledge, so surely, we can relax? He would not put us aground, would he?

Or would he?

For the course he is steering is a bit odd.

The closer we get the more obvious it is he has no intention of going anywhere near the island, the approved route, but straight across the top. I swing the lead and get 2 fathoms.

'Pete must be having kittens John.'

At which precise instant, Pete turns, throws his hands in the air, with a gesture which says all too clearly 'is he trying to wreck us?'. We collapse in uncharitable laughter. The timing is too perfect. John adds to the confusion by starting on a story about being told to swing the lead in Newlyn harbour, which he knows like the back of his hand. 'If my mates had seen me then…' and by the time we have regained our composure, we are in. Just like that.

Like the Ore, but less scary

And like the Ore, suddenly it is different.

Seductively so.

The transformation is remarkable. And to one familiar with East Coast sailing, the *Magic of the Swatchways*, the winding creeks, the saltings, the mudbanks, the curlews, the half derelict buildings peeping from the woodland, the little jetties with the occasional punt, strangely like a kind of homecoming. Albeit, unlike the East Coast, surrounded by mountains. But that, if anything heightens to sense of wonderment. The sinuous channel, the wooded bluffs, even the smell is different. You fall instantly in love with the place. For there is nothing like it anywhere on this coast. What can befall you here? A night on the mud. But not much else. At the head a small basin, a few pontoons, and a little market town to enjoy. Here *Sauntress* can lie, safe from the storms, afloat. So much kinder to a wooden boat.

Whimbrels, yes there are whimbrels, cormorants, little egrets, shags, widgeon, teal, polchard, just like, once again, those East Coast creeks, teeming with over-wintering birds, haunting and familiar cries. At anchor at the head of a creek somewhere. Frost on the decks. A naturalist's paradise. And a welcome change from that puts-hair-on-your-chest stuff outside.

And arm yourself with a book on birds. A modern one if you must, but the older ones are much more entertaining, as, for example, this:

British Birds in their Haunts, author, the Late Rev. C. A. Johns, F.L.S. first published in London, 1867, which is certainly old. What use, you may ask, is a book on British birds here in Galicia? Not much at first sight. And yet in an odd way it is. Because the value of such books is not so much the description of the birds, as the portrait the author paints of rural England in the mid nineteenth century, which, no surprise really, is *peopled by supernatural figures and haunted with dark and sinister traditions* to borrow that self-satisfied phrase from *The Times*. It is just that we seem to have forgotten. Read on:

> In the Isle of Man, a legend exists that there 'once upon a time' lived a wicked enchantress who practised her spells on the warriors of Mona, and thereby stripped the country of its chivalry (a rather ambiguous phrase). A doughty knight at length came to the rescue, and was on the point of surprising her and putting her to death, when she suddenly transformed herself into a Wren and flew through his fingers. Every year on Christmas day she is compelled to reappear in the island under the form of a Wren, with the sentence hanging over her that she is to perish by human hands. On that day, consequently, every year a grand onslaught is made by troops of idle boys and men on every Wren that can be discovered. Such as are killed are suspended from a bough of holly and carried about on triumph on the following day, the bearers singing a rude song descriptive of the previous day's hunt. This song is preserved in Quiggin's Guide to the Isle of Man as it was sung in 1853.

And yes, he has an entry on whimbrels.

Summer turns to autumn. The wind blows. The clouds scurry. The mud banks cover and uncover. Umbrellas against the Galician rain. You check the lines. Go to the market. Or to that butcher. Or to that shoemaker. The gales hustle and roar. Leaves flying, trees down.

Winter has come again.

And with it, more and yet more memories.

In the first place I chanced on the log of the *Emanuel in the Bay of Biscay 1931*, Commander Graham. It so happens that *Emanuel* is still sailing, based on the East Coast of England and is very similar in size and rig to *Sauntress*. So similar in fact that Claudia Myatt in the days when she made little postcards, illustrating this or that yacht, confused *Sauntress* with *Emanuel*. I have that card still. On a previous cruise we had followed the track of *Emanuel* in South West Ireland, the northern entrance to Baltimore harbour, wriggling through that particular gulch. And to my surprise I find we have done it again. He is working his way westward down the North Coast of Spain. And has reached the Ría de Barqueiro.

August 21st—Bar 30.05. 09.20.—Weighed, 2 rolls in mainsail. And ran down to Estaca point: thence long plug to windward, not much sea and fair progress, but poor appetites on board. Varied sail according to the wind.

16.00. Off Cabo Ortegal, Cariad just in sight to leeward but overhauling us fast.

18.00. Freshening, with rain and falling glass. Thick at times: reefed staysail.

19.30. Half way between C. Ortegal and Candelaria Pt. I decided to seek shelter whilst the going was good, and we ran back to ría Santa Marta.

21.30. Anchored off Cariño. The lie of the coast appears different from that shown on Admiralty chart no. 1755. Made good 13 miles.

August 22nd—Bar 29.70. It blew hard during the night, and we thought Cariad must be having an uncomfortable time. I subsequently heard from Carr that they had had a dirty night with five rolls in their mainsail—short sail for a Bristol Channel Pilot Cutter.

06.00—Emanuel was snubbing at her cable, so I called all hands and we got under way, well reefed down—drenching rain. Many fishing craft were sheltering in Cariño Bay which looked snug enough, but I wanted to put the bar between us and the open sea in case the wind should come seaward.

> After approaching the Isla de San Vicente, we felt our way to windward with the lead. Our least water was 1¼ fathoms (4 hours flood) but there seemed to be a channel carrying about 2 fathoms. Rounding the W headland, the water deepened, and we anchored in 4 fathoms close to the shore south of Sismundi. Usual courtesies with the local fishermen. We find everyone extremely friendly wherever we go.
>
> August 23rd—Bar 29.65. 09.30. Weighed with no 2 jib, and 3 rolls. Ran down river and crew went aloft to see better the deepest water. The bar was crossed close westward of the wreck of a large British steamer.

And that steamer, or what is left of it, is still there. Made of sterner stuff was Commander Graham, no pilot for him, feel his way to windward with the lead. Send a man up the mast, scan for the deeper water. But, they say, the channel has silted, the bar too, for the coasters of which the Admiral writes are long gone.

Commander Graham was right to clear out of Cariño. For the fourth time, winter storms have breached the harbour wall there. It is not a safe anchorage, despite appearances. For Cariño faces East. It is protected from the West or Northwest, you would think, by the great headland that is Cabo Ortegal and those needle rocks, the Aguillones. All a chimera. For when the swell rolls in, driven by one of those winter gales, of protection there is none.

'Ah' said Manolo, retired mariner—Ortigueira having its fair share of such, ready to gossip, very Galician. By which I mean this: in the first place he demands, but demands (actually more than that. Do you know what he said? 'Sell me *Sauntress* and I will give her back to you') to see *Sauntress*, under full sail, in the *ría*. For he remembers the Grand Banks, those schooners what is more. (No, not possible, but perhaps it is). Not to mention this, his home *ría*, in the last days of sail. In the second he plies us with drink after drink. Wind changed? Turn of the tide. As the conversation meanders, two old geezers gossiping if you like. That shared something, unspoken for all that we are talking. And was insulted when I offered to pay for a round. No, not insulted so much as bemused. For I was breaking the rules, or the mood. And in the third came *my house is your house.* And he means it. A little drunk? Of course, we were a little drunk. Firm handshake. Reluctant parting. For this has all the hallmarks of an all-nighter.

'Now' he says, 'I will explain. You would think the place protected from the west by Cabo Ortegal.' (Which is precisely what I think, hence the question). 'You see. Here the Cantabrian Sea and the Atlantic meet.' Nothing more to be said. Causing what the Admiral would surely call 'abnormal waves.'

Then you remember a summer message from yacht *Larry*, just down the coast in Ferrol. Her skipper wrote:

> As we dropped anchor in a quiet little bay opposite Ferrol one of the grandsons said, 'this is paradise!' And they immediately set forth in our 3 dinghies!

And how right he is. It is a kind of paradise. For there is something almost magical about that anchorage. Hard to put your finger on. The view after all is not all that inspiring. Cranes mostly. But turn your back on that, and you are looking at something completely different, jungle, green, green, green. Down to the water's edge green. With yellow sand. And half collapsed houses. And a backwater. And a stream at the head. And an avenue of plane trees. Shuttered villas. Sunless. But not at midday. Uncomfortable in a north-easterly. Tantalizing and mysterious.

Our secret place.

The true cruising yacht, and *Larry* is certainly that, has a habit of popping up in the most unexpected ways. Indeed, the best kind are there in the evening and gone at dawn. Ribadeo and it was like that. Tall ships over and they appeared in Redes, on Pete's mooring, where, rowing out stealthily, I surprised her skipper, immersed in reading.

'Oh hello.'

'Like it here?'

'We are loving it.'

And no wonder. As a place for grandchildren to play in the dinghies, it was ideal.

And again, they were gone.

The next time we saw them was by land.

Holed up in a yard in Corunna, a long dusty walk to anywhere much, they took the FEVE[*] up to where we live to chew the cud and paella for a few hours.

And again, they were gone.

Will-o'-the wisp like.

Until our paths should cross again.

And should they ever choose to put pen to paper, what a story that would be. But they keep quiet about what they have done, the miles they have sailed, the places they have been. Across the table, yes. Otherwise no.

So, no it is.

---

[*] The FEVE is a narrow-gauge railway which runs from Ferrol to San Sebastian. Four times a day. Very slow and very appealing. Not quite one of the great railway journeys of the world. But then again. All the way along the coast, shouldering its way through woodlands, sudden glimpses of absurdly blue sea. Umpteen halts. A delight.

Don Vicente Tofiño de San Miguel and Los Aguillones

In 1805 Captain William Brown commanded the Ajax, of 74 guns, and was present in the action of Cape Finisterre on 22 July; [fought in fog—no wind worthy of the name] but by bearing up at the critical moment of the attack, he weakened the English van, and as the cause of the unsatisfactory result of the action, he left the Ajax and returned to England. He was therefore absent from Trafalgar, where the Ajax was commanded by Lieutenant Pilford. Captain Tylor and Captain Brown must have known each other, might have been close and maybe Brown gave Tyler his charts when the former went home in disgrace after the Cape Finisterre debacle.

Catalogue of an auction sale of sea charts, Bonham's

A n odd way of exploring history. But there we are.
Interesting though this little cameo of an unsatisfactory (from the British standpoint) naval engagement might be, it is not for that, that it is reproduced here. It is for the charts. Because the charts in question were not British Admiralty charts, but Spanish Admiralty Charts. Prepared under the supervision of Don Vicente Tofiño de San Miguel (1732-1795) a contemporary of Captain Cook (1728-1779). He produced two sets of sailing directions,

respectively for the Mediterranean coast of Spain and Northern Africa (1787) and the *Derrotero de las Costas de España en el Océano Atlántico etc* (1789). In each case with accompanying charts.

Which, if to be found aboard a British man of war, would perhaps have been seized from a Spanish prize, Just, as in earlier times *Drake and the Filibusters* to use Don Vicente Tofiño de San Miguel's expression, seized upon the Spanish charts aboard the *Galéon* for what he calls the Southern Sea (meaning the Spanish overseas empire), as being superior to any other. In his introduction to the *Derrotero*, he remarks that all this exploration of the furthest parts of the globe had produced the curious circumstance that these far-flung corners were better understood than *the continent which we inhabit*. (A strangely modern comment).

Which he made it his business to rectify.

This is the period of Harrison's chronometer, *the watch made by Mr Berthoud.*[*] (Not just Harrison as we are led to believe, for others were hot on his heels if not more), triangulation, theodolites, meridian altitude sights, eclipses of the first and second satellites of Jupiter, lunars, the sounding lead, the sextant, the thermometer and all the paraphernalia of 18th century survey work. And fathoms, (fathoms being *brazas* which is to say the span of a man's outstretched arms) and cables, and miles and leagues.

Whether you be a Spanish mariner or English.

Such was the value of these charts and sailing directions that an English translation was published under the title *España Marítima* by W. Faden, Geographer to His Majesty and to His Royal Highness the Prince Regent, London 1812. The preface reads in part:

> From the High Estimation of this Nautical Survey of the Coast of Spain, and

---

[*] In 1773, Ferdinand Berthoud published his *Traité des horloges marines contenant la théorie, la construction, la main-d'œuvre de ces machines et la manière de les éprouver, pour parvenir par leur moyen, à la rectification des cartes marines et à la détermination des longitudes en mer.* This treatise was a first, detailing all the parts required for building a sea clock. It helped seal the reputation of Berthoud's work, with respect to his competitors in longitude at sea research, such as Harrison and Pierre Le Roy

the great difficulty in procuring it, several Distinguished Officers of the Royal Navy repeatedly urged the necessity of printing an English Edition for the Public Service.

We need perhaps to remind ourselves of the old usages. *The League contains three nautical or Maritime Miles, Twenty Leagues being one degree.* Followed by:

ADVERTISMENT

The fathom adopted in this work has been the English, with the exception only of those used in the charts of Ferrol and Corunna where the Spanish fathom has been used, which like the English fathom contains six feet; but as the standard foot of Spain is somewhat shorter than the English foot, the difference between the Spanish fathom and the English fathom comes to be considerable.

As to quite why the Spanish foot should be shorter than the English foot? Another time, maybe.
Now to Don Vicente Tofiño de San Miguel, and *Los Aguillones*:

At S 81°30′W six miles and eight tenths from the Punta Estaca is the Cape of the Aguillones which is high and precipitous. The name Aguillones is given to the islets which are to the NNW of the Cape, interconnected, but leaving a pass, albeit it narrow, between these and between the Cape.

All of which serves to introduce a little outing, courtesy Alvaro. Born in a hamlet with views over the Ría de Ortigueira, owner of a small sailing boat emblazoned with *Quieres Vela?* meaning *Fancy a sail?*, he runs excursions for those that do.
And one day he had room on board for Luis and me.
We boarded at Espasante. Tourist attraction the pig of Espasante, which wanders the village all summer, to be auctioned in the autumn to pay the costs of a fiesta, and then sacrificed. But the pig seldom is. Sentimentality (surpris-

ingly for Galicia) winning the day.

The wind was south, force 7. Which heralds an approaching low. We all scrambled down the ladder on the quayside, to be arranged, on cushions, in the cockpit in that 'now let the fun begin' kind of way.

Which it did.

For force 7 notwithstanding, all sail was hoisted, and off, on our ear, we went. Alvaro gave me the wheel. For the boat had wheel, not tiller, steering. But, being hydraulically assisted, the steering had no 'feel'. Which means you twirl the wheel this way or that and wait to see what happens. A very erratic course.

Destination, Los Aguillones.

Obeying the instinct which says the further from land the better, I took her well clear, in a rising wind and sea. Alvaro reefs. High time too. And being in command gives the order, *Go about now*. We are perhaps a mile off the Aguillones and fractionally upwind. And having gone about are now bearing down on the Cape at a rate of knots. Quite a bit of spray around. The Aguillones in our lee. Frankly at this stage I am having kittens. There is no margin for error, accident, or anything much. So, when he says, 'You can give me the helm now,' I am only too glad. If he wants to wreck his boat, so be it. We do not of course wreck, or I would not be writing this. Instead we are heading for *a pass, albeit narrow,* in the words of that Spanish 18th century hydrographer, Don Vicente, between these by now imposing rocks, width, half a cable. At most. Full of pot markers. Wonderful fishing here.

The guests are certainly getting their money's worth. For a closer view of the *Aguillones* you could not ask for. In fact, you could practically lean over and grab a mussel or two.

We shoot through into calm waters. Potter around a bit. And head for Espasante. Only it is not Espasante. It is the bar at Ortigueira. Half an hour after low water.

Surely, he is not going to…?

But he is.

It is not showing off. Alvaro is not that kind of person. It is not incompetence. For he knows his stuff and his waters. It is just that Alvaro is Alvaro. And this time he does enter next to the island. For the bar is breaking badly.

What was that about Ortigueira being 'the town where nothing ever happens?'

They clearly haven't heard of Alvaro.

27

The Winter List

Quite a lot of sailing is actually dreaming.
    Just being aboard.
Pump her. Count the strokes.

She is not far away. The distance it takes to smoke a cigarette whilst driving. Stop in Mera de Abaixo. For some reason they have the best bread for miles around. It's the water, says Luis. Where do you come from they ask? They call me *El Irlandés* I answer. They keep a tally of each thing they sell in a notebook. Incredibly old fashioned. They are used to me by now.

Mera de Abaixo, Mera de Arriba. Upper and lower. In fact, the other way around. For it is hilly here. Up where we are, head in the clouds. Down below, signs it is clearing. And here the wetlands start. For Mera de Abaixo is the very head of the *ría*. The brook under the road bridge noisy after the rains. Low water and acres of mud, a silver thread the water. Unruffled at times. Like today.

I like the way the view unfolds. Slowly at first, and then, as the road swings around, the great hump that is Cabo Ortegal, summit festooned with masts, and wind turbines, but you learn to shut those out of your vision. Clean energy. Which would be more convincing if it were not for the fact that the energy which goes into making one such monster, not to mention transporting it, giant convoy belching diesel fumes, (that is one blade on its way somewhere), erecting it, maintaining it, far exceeds anything it is ever likely to generate. Or so I suspect.

Such thoughts heretical.

Step across *Martlet*, who curtseys hardly at all, step aboard *Sauntress*, and, yes, she curtseys in welcome, undo the covers, fold back, and step below.

Little light green?

Good, the batteries are on full charge. Months it took to crack that conundrum, but we have it now. Solar panel, charge controller, four-way switch and those two batteries, under the chart table seat. A good wiring job you have done, said Julian, Luis' cousin, as he finished the bits I could not. Sweating rather, for he is a large man. A large man in a small boat.

Later we will have *pulpo*. And he won't let me pay. One of three bars in the square. On one side of which the 'marina', the other the bars, but we have our favourite. 'Remember my name?' says Veronica. 'Yes' I reply, 'Veronica.' And who is it in the town who talks to me in French? In the ironmonger's. Born in Switzerland. Very Galician that. The diaspora. 'Hola Martin.' 'Hola Alberto,' or 'Hola Estrella.' I thought them husband and wife. Gales of laughter. Best butcher for just about everything. But that is Ortigueira for you. A proper market town. The butcher, the baker, the candle-stick maker. Not that, but candles for alters. Dead cheap. And cathedral quality.

And sure enough, every Thursday, in that square, it is market day.

Scrub the decks, bucket after bucket of sea water. And, it would seem, no deck leaks now. You did that job in the last of the dry spells. All around the edge of the cabin. Where there used to be little puddles on the shelf below. Run your hand under the carlin. Dry.

Brought the hardboard? Yes. Start on the patterns. For in your wilder flights of fancy you see your ship hurled on her side, in some great storm, cabin sides stove in. And having allowed your mind to visualize such a disaster, the other part of that same mind says. Do something about it. Which is what I am doing now.

Hanging knees. Three pairs. Giving a kind of cathedral effect in the cabin. But giving strength. Strength where it is needed.

Up to Mr *Jamón*, on a stormy day. Three enormous planks. With curved grain. From which, slowly, for the wood is hard, your saw not of the best, you cut out those knees. Then 'offer up' in the parlance, mark with a pencil, measure the bevel, take home, and adjust. And so on. *Ad infinitum.*

Or, sometimes, just dreaming. Or remembering.

> A keen owner of a very little yacht, if he have sufficient leisure, may derive pleasure and amusement from doing his own painting and varnishing.

That's Claud Worth talking. At his patronizing best. Though he probably did not realise it. But I do 'derive pleasure and amusement,' though not much of that in the forepeak as I struggle first with dust and later with fumes. Lovely fresh cream paint when done.

'Half past seven in the School of Gaiteros.'

'Alright Alvaro.'

There was a problem. The 'marina' had gone bust. Been pocketing the money and forgetting to pay *Portos de Galicia*. A shadowy organization. (What's new?) Whose representative, one Javier, had announced, cool as you please, that we would all have to pay twice. 'All' meaning mostly the owners of small punts, fishermen to a man, horny handed sons of, well not the soil, but certainly of Galicia. Except that contentious Dutchman. What is it about Dutchmen? The one in the hills got himself murdered. And this one too if he is not careful. 'Objectionable man,' said Alvaro.

We shuffle off up the hill to the School of Gaiteros, where there is to be an action committee. (Shades of this and that). Except that they have forgotten the key. Which rather deflates the revolutionary atmosphere. For it is difficult to harangue in a corridor, draughty, interminable, one man, for reasons not apparent, hiding in a cupboard. And we all say yes. Or something. And I, the only outsider in the place, try to blend into a corner, longing for a fag. Next meeting next Saturday. That was three months ago. And still nothing.

After the storms the beach is covered with seaweed. Remember to take a couple of stout plastic bags and Luis has nutrients for the garden, *very Galician that,* which it is. In the 1920s an American, Ruth Matilda Anderson, commissioned by the Hispanic Society of America, spent several years in

Spain photographing, people mostly, fishermen, farmers, the women-folk, a collection remarkable not only for the quality of the photographs, but for the near medieval world she recorded. Including ox carts, laden with kelp, to fertilise the land, very poor soil too, up on the *Costa de la Muerte*.

But my goodness the *cestas*, wicker baskets, carried on the head of the womenfolk. Overflowing with this and that, including, if memory serves, a pheasant (in Lugo market, that in 1960). And you realise that Spain, medieval rural Spain at any rate, has been yanked into the 21st century in the space of less than one hundred years. Luis would probably say fifty years. Given the *dictadura*. No wonder so much persists of the old ways.

And of the old courtesies.

Especially those.

28

The Stranding of the Howe and Other High Victorian Tales

ADVERTISMENT

The fathom adopted in this work has been the English, with the exception only of those used in the charts of Ferrol and Corunna where the Spanish fathom has been used, which like the English fathom contains six feet; but as the standard foot of Spain is somewhat shorter than the English foot, the difference between the Spanish fathom and the English fathom comes to be considerable.

Remember? Remember *gentle reader*, one could almost say, given the distinctly Kiplingesque flavour of what follows.

For we are drawn, by the most unlikely thread into precisely that world, courtesy a fleeting reference in Messing About in Boats (John R. Muir— Lodestar Books 2016). The story John Muir is telling relates to the loss of the *Montagu* on Shutter Rock, Lundy island, in thick fog in May 1906, a piece of naval incompetence and the most important disaster, he remarks *since the stranding of the Howe in Ferrol.*

Understandably perhaps, there is not much to be found in English language sources on what sounds suspiciously like an embarrassing incident. Better to draw a discreet veil. Turn, however to the Spanish sources and that self-same veil is ripped aside, and mercilessly so, in the shape of a lengthy monograph, one of a series published in *La Revista General de la Marina* (Spanish Naval Review) by Luis Jar Torre, Master Mariner and Full Commander in the Spanish Navy who sets to work with gusto and understandably with a degree of *schadenfreude*. But facts are facts. And the facts, in outline, are these.

The *Howe* was conceived at a time when money was short and when the invention of the torpedo had called into question the very existence of the battleship—*any money spent on battleships was money wasted*—and in answer to our old enemy the French, with their *Terrible* class. A sort of rather reluctant, something must be done, but on a budget type reaction which, so quintessentially British in its approach, produced the *Admiral* class, limited to 10,000 tons.

Over to Luis Jar Torre, under the title *A Plantagenet in the Court of Ferrol*—a reference to the ancestry of the Captain of HMS *Howe*, Alexander Plantagenet Hastings, distant forbear Henry III. Or, whimsically Robin Hood.

> In 1880 [he writes] naval breech loading gunnery was in its infancy and one of the greatest headaches associated with this series [the Admiral class] was the incapacity of foundries to meet the delivery dates for the principal armament which so delayed the commissioning of the ships as to render them obsolete. In the case of the Howe, the keel was laid in 1882 in the Pembroke shipyard. She was launched three years later but could not be incorporated into the fleet until her main armament was installed in 1890, a lapse of time during which the triple expansion engine was introduced (greater steaming range), nickel steel armour plating had been invented (improved protection), and rapid-fire guns had been introduced. The 'Admiral' class were not able to benefit from all of these advances but to the second and the third of the series, the Rodney and the Howe, a number of ad hoc modifications were made to improve the armour plating, and they were given four guns of 13,5' closing the gap with the French. But, since these changes added 810 tons and the dimensions of the vessel were unchanged, Archimedes presented his bill in the shape of 46cm more draught, which immersed the armoured belt to a

depth of doubtful usefulness, but, phlegmatically, it was felt that since the ship would not enter combat until a good portion of the coal had been consumed, the problem would solve itself.

The upshot was an extremely wet ship, sailing *submerged* but, to damn with faint praise, '*they* [the Admiral class] *were better fighting ships than those before them,*' which is Rear Admiral Seymour, of whom more later, speaking. The *Howe*, when at last commissioned was duly incorporated into the Channel Squadron which in turn, in November 1892, was to be found anchored in Corunna Bay on a courtesy visit. Flagship the *Royal Sovereign*, the squadron under the command of Admiral Fairfax, second in command Seymour, whilst the captain of the *Howe* was A. P. Hastings and that of the *Royal Sovereign* Hammill

There were eight battleships in the squadron, but one was sent south and a second fouled her anchor and was left *looking at her own reflection,* this is Luis Jar Torre speaking once more. Which left six. The *Royal Sovereign*, the *Howe*, the *Immortalité*, the *Anson*, the *Rodney* and the *Bellona*.

All destined to pay a courtesy visit to the Captain General of Ferrol. Described by Luis Jar Torre thus: *at that period the Royal Navy suffered from an exhibitionist tendency which led them to cow potential 'clients' with elaborate ritual dances, which necessarily included anchoring in formation.* There is, however, the small matter of bringing the Channel Squadron, in open formation—that is each ship separated by four cables—into, according to Seymour, *the finest naval port I know.* The idea was a visit of three hours, but little did Seymour know…

> Every mariner knows the old saying 'Britannia rules the waves' but nowhere is it written that 'waves' include 'tides' and if Laplace [Laplace's theory of ocean tides] is not wrong, high water in Ferrol was at 1303 which would mean that the Channel Squadron would be obliged to enter [the narrows] with a flood tide under them which in places could reach two knots.

So writes L.J. Torre. (What was that about *schadenfreude?*)

Enter our old friend Don Vicente Tofiño de San Miguel, that Spanish cartographer, contemporary of Captain Cooke, whose charts and sailing directions were held in such high esteem etc. For it was his chart, in the shape of Admiralty Chart 80 upon which Fairfax proposed to rely, Spanish fathoms and all. But not, it seems, the sailing directions, where Don Tofiño has this to say:

> When the tides are near the Equinox, the current runs with much violence in the narrow part which means that with such tides, as indeed with any tide, it is advisable to enter or leave, be it at high water or low water, one hour beforehand, so as to stem the [flood or ebb]…
>
> *[my translation]*

Fairfax had other ideas. Remarking that in relation to entering a strange port such as Ferrol that it was a matter *of extreme simplicity to British seamen accustomed to handle such ships* and, for good measure, *the spectacle of a British squadron of powerful twin screw battleships waiting outside Ferrol Harbour, because of a tide which sailing ships and single screw steamships of heavy draught had found no difficulty with in the past, would have been scarcely worthy of the tradition of British seamanship.*

Harrumph. Or, better, hubris.

Thus at 10.50 am on 2nd November 1892, the squadron, *Royal Sovereign* in the van, with steam for 10 knots but proceeding at 7 knots, was between the two headlands flanking the entrance to the channel (and with a couple of hours of flood still to run), when a rowing boat with two individuals at the oars and one steering was observed, and thinking that the individual might be the port captain, speed was reduced to 4 knots. But upon seeing that the man was not wearing a uniform, it was concluded that *the man steering was a pilot, and he was waved out of the way,* speed increased to 6 knots, Hammill (captain of the Royal Sovereign) declaring that *he would not have permitted a Spanish pilot to take charge of the flagship Royal Sovereign.* Admiral Fairfax went further, stating *if we had employed local pilots the Howe would probably have had companions in misfortune.*

Verbatim.

As for the *extreme simplicity,* there is an element of truth, at least until you reach the two forts Castillo San Felipe to port and. Castillo de Palma to starboard a few cables beyond. Here there was (it has since been dynamited) a shoal patch now called, mischievously *El bajo inglés*, originally and more logically *Bajo de la Palma*, with which the navigating officer of the *Howe*, D.L. Dixon, was intimately acquainted, having been aboard HMS *Sultan*, when she grounded, a few years earlier. (To call this shoal *El bajo inglés*, says J. L. Torre, is a bit rich, since it had been 'discovered' by a Spanish armoured frigate, the *Tetuán*, on sea trials, well before the HMS Sultan *made its acquaintance*). At which point it dawns. This man has a cracking sense of humour and a distinctly sharp tongue to boot. Which is why he is such good value.

The avoidance of this shoal was therefore what J.L. Torre calls the *plato fuerte* of the entire evolution, which the flagship, HMS *Royal Sovereign*, managed by a whisker.

> The chief naval officer of that port (surely the Captain General) on seeing the squadron enter 'was surprised that the leading ship did not strike on the rock herself.'

Consider. The squadron was entering on a flood tide, near springs, where to quote Tofiño, *the current runs with much violence*, something with which the Admiralty pilot concurs, *3. 71. In the narrows.... the tidal streams.... attain a maximum rate at springs of about 4 knots.* Thus squirted, and no other word will do, out of the narrows like a cork out of a bottle. And with about as much control.

What is more, they were relying on a chart first published in 1789 albeit corrected to 1886, with depths in Spanish fathoms (smaller than British fathoms), with no pilot, and trusting to compass course, apparently suspect, clearing bearings, back bearings, the latter obstructed by funnels, masts and quite possibly smoke, and in terms of keeping station, the sextant. And in the case of HMS *Howe*, by all accounts grossly underpowered, deep in the water, a bitch to steer, all in all a recipe for the disaster about to unfold.

The evolution, which, despite all, came off for HMS *Royal Sovereign*, but not for HMS *Howe*, was this. Clear the first fort, Castillo de San Felipe, and turn hard to port into the bay beyond, thus skirting *El bajo inglés*, and once clear turn hard to starboard, aiming for Mugardos across the bay, to clear the last danger, Punta del Vispón and another off-lying shoal patch called *Bajo Pereiro*.

To resume, we turn to, of all places, the Antipodes, whose press appears somewhat hostile—the *New Zealand Evening Post* 7th November 1892 remarking sourly that the *Howe struck in broad daylight*—whilst the *South Australian Register* of 27th February 1893, resorting to Shakespeare, (Macbeth Act IV scene 1) gives us this image:

> The Royal Sovereign passed the Palmas and rounded the shoal at a safe distance. The Howe behind him, determined to make assurance double sure, and rounded the shoal outside the leading ship's wake.

Assurance double sure it was not. Here is Hastings speaking:

> The land was then well open and the ship's head was pointing towards the centre of Mugardos village in a south-easterly direction. Both the navigating commander and myself were satisfied the ship was then clear of Pereiro shoal by clearing marks, and being, as we believed, in a perfectly safe position, with her head pointing for entering the harbour, the helm was put amidships.

The *Royal Sovereign*, meanwhile, having cleared the dangers, was faced by two buoys not marked on the chart, where she proposed the squadron should anchor, and gave the signal for the remainder of the squadron to reduce speed. Apparently, *Not knowing whether the anchorage was clear, I deemed it prudent for a short time to reduce the speed of the squadron to 4 knots.* But it seems that he gave no such order, merely *reduce speed* without reference to the rest of the squadron. Whatever the truth, signal 25 *by an error… was hoisted* and then *I ordered it be hauled down before it was answered.*

But the damage was done.

For D. L. Dixon, navigating officer aboard the *Howe*, had already noticed, by sextant measurement, that the distance had come down to three cables instead of four and Hastings gave the order *Go as slow as possible viz, 22 revolutions* equivalent to 3 knots in the presence of a current of 2 knots, which given her unorthodox course was enough to convert her position from one of flirting with danger to one of running aground. *At 1125 / the ship struck / being more than half a cable from the shore / the chart giving me seven or eight fathoms / and there being a rise at this time of at least 11 feet due to tide.*

The *Howe* attempted to get off with the engines full astern. But desisted when the bridge was informed that the two port boiler rooms were flooded and the fires out. Which was perhaps just as well, for a subsequent inspection by the ship's carpenter found that a longitudinal bulkhead as well as the watertight doors were *leaking freely*. And *that if the ship slipped into deep water she would probably not float.*

Anchors were put out (no mean operation with the ship impaled on a rock) to prevent the *Howe* slipping into deep water. And there, until 30th March of the following year, she remained (the rock on which she was impaled was dynamited, the hull patched up and the Howe re-floated to be put in dry dock in Ferrol).

The Spanish press had a field day:

> …accusing our colleagues [this is Luis Jar Torre speaking as a fellow mariner] in the Victorian navy of a degree of arrogance,' adding, for good measure, 'only for English mariners are there imperfections in the charts and lighthouses, since where others navigate in perfect safety they wreck daily— the Spanish Government has no need of a fresh survey of the entrance to the bay of Ferrol, nor to amend the chart since this chart contains neither error nor omission.

Things, however, were not quite so straightforward.
As the Courts Martial showed.
Hastings loyally stood by his navigating officer:

> A reliable and competent officer and in no way to blame for what had occurred. I have shown by several witnesses the unexpectedness of the direction and force of the current—the flood tide was running three to four knots—I cannot be held to blame / for striking a rock not marked on the chart.

He then imprudently pointed the finger at Hammill (the captain of the *Royal Sovereign*), claiming that the unexpected slowing of the *Royal Sovereign* momentarily distracted him, and thus impugning his Admiral. Most unwise. The Court Martial found that the Howe

> had run aground on a sandy shoal [sic] unknown at the time and that the chart shows seven Spanish fathoms of water above the shoal at low water.
>
> The Court has much pleasure in returning you your swords with your reputations untarnished.

That at least was the verdict of the Court Martial on Hastings and his navigating officer. Their Lordships of the Admiralty were however not best pleased, and Seymour, in his memoirs, (*My Naval Career and Travels*, by Admiral of the Fleet the Right Honourable Sir Edward Hobart Seymour, London, Smith Elder and Co. 1911) is categoric:

> Her captain was a very good officer, also young for his position, already distinguished, and with the best of service prospects. The result was his professional ruin. I only mention this, not so much to blame him, it might have happened to others, but to show how precarious is the career of a naval officer, and how one minute's error (even in peace time) may mean professional ruin, or the loss of the ship.

Seymour's naval career spanned the years 1852 (when he entered the navy aged 12) to 1910 when aged 70, he was placed on the retired list. The memoirs are, as might be expected, a first-hand account of naval engagements from the Crimean War to the Boxer rebellion and beyond, written in the style befitting the period and attitudes of the time, most of it what can only be described as High Victorian adventure, appearing under such titles as *Disturbances on the Bonny River*, cannibalism, slave ships, pirates, shipwrecks and tales of derring do, the Indian mutiny, and so on. A good read simply as an adventure story, in the mould of Kipling or John Buchan, though rather more *de haut en bas*. But now and again something stands out as, for example, when he writes of the Crimean War, Odessa 1854, where you find this, the swan-song of the Nelsonian navy:

> A pretty episode resembling olden days took place in the Arethusa, a 50-gun sailing frigate, then commanded by Captain W. R. Mends, standing in under sail and engaging the outer batteries; this being, I believe, the last time that an English man-of-war was ever in action under sail.

Or this remarkable, not to say baffling, passage:

> I remember one day a French line-of-battle ship looming out of the fog close to our starboard beam, both ships barely moving and ours just clearing her by putting men in our paddle-wheels to turn them, the wheels being of course disconnected from the engines.

The ship is HMS *Terrible*, the largest steam-powered wooden paddle wheel frigate afloat at the time. How was it done? It is a conundrum. There you are about, apparently, to collide with a French line-of-battle ship. You have time, it seems, to disconnect the paddle wheels from the engine and then 'put men in them' meaning what? By sheer weight of numbers perhaps, the wheels begin to turn, but then what? For as the wheels start to turn, your men are in for a dip, or do they leap nimbly from lower blade to upper? Or start in the paddle box and leap for the rail. And is this a 'recognised manoeuvre' lost to posterity? For surely you have no time to explain what is required. And all in time to avoid a collision.

PhD discourse needed.

Meanwhile, the Boxer rebellion.

Our man is now in command of the China Station where having digested, *Chusan Island, Occupation of Wei-hai-wei, Nagasaki, Hankow, Nankin, Hong Kong, Manilla, Formosa, H.M.S. Bonaventure grounding, Vladivostok, Russian Tartary Convict Prison, Japan, The Yang-tse Rapids, H.R.H. Prince Henry of Prussia, Siam, Borneo,* by way of aperitif (and what a wonderful life it must have been), he finds himself in command of a desperate expedition to the relief of the legation in Peking, by train, lines blown by the Boxer rebels and repaired under fire, North-West frontier style, leading the combined naval forces of no less than eight nationalities British, German, Russian, French, United States (fresh from relieving Spain of the Philippines—and Cuba for that matter—a decidedly imperial venture for this allegedly anti-imperial country), Japanese, Italian and Austrian, when all at once comes this thoughtful, one might almost say humble, and decidedly *not* High Victorian, passage:

> Let me here remark as follows. The general history of our dealings with China has been that we have forced ourselves undesired upon them and into their country. I believe we are too apt to forget this, and not to make those allowances in consequence. But Crabbe's well-known lines beginning
> 'How is it men, when they in judgment sit
> On the same faults now censure now acquit'
> apply to nations as much as to men. I might easily enlarge on this subject by dilating on the religious question, on the opium trade, on the war of 1840, and on events both before and after that; but that is not my theme.

Thus spake...

To revert to the unfinished story of the *Howe*. Next came the Court Martial of Admiral Fairfax. An irritated Fairfax. The charge was that *He selected a time when a strong flood tide was running and when he was guided by a chart which was principally founded on a Spanish survey in 1789.* The Hydrographer of the Navy contended that the chart *contained imperfections and that such an incomplete chart could not be considered trustworthy in its details,* adding that the difficulties *were considerably increased on November 2, and demanded considerable skill.* Fairfax, one suspects by this time near incandescent with rage, mounts a rousing defence (*encendido elogio* is the phrase used in Spanish) of the chart, amended in 1873 and again in 1886, as *compared with the charts of other Spanish ports / is of a distinctly superior class,* before poking Hastings in the eye (a Spanish expression). *It is not the duty of a following ship in a winding channel to follow every slight deviation in the course of the leader.*

Once again, the Court had much pleasure........

And as to the accuracy or otherwise of that chart? One MP apparently remarked: *She struck not on an isolated unknown rock, as was suggested, but upon the mainland of Spain.*

Which rather says it all.

There is, however, a rather nice footnote to all this. Fairfax's second in command, Rear Admiral Seymour—destined, as we have seen for greater things—was left behind to pick up the pieces, so to speak, keep an eye on and eventually re-float the *Howe*. He remained 229 days in Ferrol and records his excellent relationship with the Captain General of Ferrol, V.A. Carranza, *a dignified Spanish Don, speaking English well and always assisting us in every way he could,* not to mention a relaxed atmosphere, no longer under the eye of Fairfax, nor subject to the rigours of navigating *submerged,* but instead *He* [the Captain General] *and his Señora had a reception every Thursday evening to which some of us always went.* Adding, wistfully *There were many ladies there, and our acquaintance among them was large, but among them not one spoke English and only five spoke French.*

Ooh—la-la. It has to be. So *fin de siècle.*

29

In Sheltered Waters

Goodness how they love long words here. Explosive cyclogenesis for example. And what is wrong with the old terms, secondary low (not quite the same but even so), that nasty sudden and vicious little storm which comes almost from nowhere, something of a speciality of this coast. Cedeira, for example, winds gusting—you can look it up—at 143km per hour (which is 77 knots or, on the Beaufort scale, F12).

And that, in winter, is not unusual.

Which is why, tucked up in Santa Marta de Ortigueira, yes, even there, the howling storms, trees down, roads converted to rivers, you wonder. And go down to check, yet again, the lines. Pump her, for the rain, stair rods rain, gets in somehow, but in the autumn, those last few weeks when all pauses, the crowds gone, winter at bay, you can enjoy the *ría*, one last time.

Sheltered waters. Made for playing.

The protagonist this time is not Alvaro, but Tino, who appears and disappears like some will-o'-the-wisp, big yacht skipper when away, overgrown schoolboy when here. And water, always the water, anything that floats, as for example this:

'When are you going to finish that rig?'

'Soon Tino, soon.'

'Good. You can launch at Mera. I want to see how she goes.'

So did I.

It was, in truth, a bit of a lash up. Inherited sail, far too big, inherited oddments, adapted more in hope than expectation, for dinghy sailor I am not, but thought it might be fun. If not for me, then for others.

'*Qué bonito!*' (ships being male here, not female).

We are at the water's edge at the top of the ría. The dinghy has been manhandled into and out of Tino's distinctive bright orange van. It floats demure. Luis seated on a rock, holding the painter, with a resigned expression on his face, which says all too clearly...

Rather be fishing.

The '*qué bonito!*' came from a Galician with her young grandsons, enjoying the last of the summer sun. They had a large inflatable dragon. She paddled in the shallows, skirts hitched. A secluded spot reached down a track winding through the apple orchards. The little red variety, sharp and juicy. A couple of month's work in the autumn. Apple picking. Like they used to do in Kent. Alvaro does that. Supplementing *Quieres Vela*.

In the offing, Tino's boat. Nice lines. Back from Falmouth.

All rather bucolic in short. Lost in nostalgia.

'And you made the bote? *Mira chicos*.' (look boys).

Tino and I exchange glances.

'You see what I mean. This place is dead, but just see the reaction.'

Tino is right. The dinghy has stirred a memory. Not a sail on the *ría* now. And his plan is to change all that. With that house at the head, and his own boat here too, why not start a sailing school, and then a wooden boatyard, and then...

They all go for a sail, break this and that and return laughing, a bit wet, exhibiting, oh dear, so much for the boatbuilder, broken mast heel, broken rudder pintle, a bailer, in constant use—better *Sauntress* really. So you take the wreckage home, send it up into the rafters and think of something else.

Tino, God the man is exhausting, now has his eye on *Sauntress*. Pester, pester, leaving soon, tides good tomorrow, won't be back until spring...

'Come on Martin! It won't take long to bend the sails and I will help you unbend them afterwards.'

Still bridling. All too difficult. No I don't want to. And anyway how do we get back in again? In a word, pathetic. What has happened to the enthusiasm of youth?

At which point, and shamed, he wins.

'Let go forward!'

'Ah, I like a clear command.'

Thank you Tino. Nothing like a bit of flattery. Not to mention cracking of the whip. For *of course* I am dying for a sail. Sailing out of or into a marina is frowned on, perhaps understandably. But here, bowsprit pointing at the harbour's mouth (for the 'marina' is within a harbour), wind astern, you have only to set the foresail, release the last line and she will gather way. And when outside, whip up the main, port your helm and you are on a reach down the channel, time to add the jib and hand over to the champing-at-the-bit, bubbling-with-enthusiasm, Tino. 'Tis his outing after all.

'So light on the helm—so responsive.'

'Well Tino, no propeller you see.'

'Ah, of course.'

The *ría* slowly unfolded in all its seductive beauty, great hills tumbling down to the wetlands, little buildings peeping from trees, a harder puff had *Sauntress* heel and the grin grew. Thank God, sailing again. Tino at the helm by all means, but sailing.

'Helm alee.'

'Back the foresail?'

'No Tino. She does not need it.'

He expounds for a while on the run of the channel and the back marks you need to line up, church tower inevitably, with something. Chatting all the time.

'They were in tears you know. *Costas* (the Coastal Authority) came and told them to take everything away.'

Tino is talking here about the *carpinteiros de ribeira* (which translates literally as shoreside carpenters but means wooden boatbuilders). All gone now. Although the wooden punts, old style, all virtually identical, flat bottomed and heavy, have not. Grizzled old men, and not so old too, fishing, fishing,

fishing the ría. And when *Sauntress* was ashore, gossiping, gossiping and gossiping again. Or tapping the hull, 'what timber?'—'pitch pine'—'good timber that.'

The breeze strengthened.

'Over there is a hole where you can anchor.'

I had wondered about that, disliking marinas as I do. But even in here, even in this sheltered and largely tidal estuary, not ready for that yet. Lay a mooring. She would be more comfortable on a mooring.

'See the mast?'

Tino had found an old stone basin in which his yacht was now lying at the foot of a ramp and above the ramp a shed, a boatbuilder's shed on all of which he hoped to lay his hands, a year or so of negotiation with *Costas*.

'We can go close in here.'

True, but the wind boxed the proverbial compass under the trees whilst *Sauntress*, obedient as ever, followed it round, bowsprit swinging, swinging, swinging till we came clear again.

'A short tack here. Ready?'

'But she tacks through 90°. Gaffers are not supposed to do that.'

Flattering, but untrue. Close winded by all means, but not all that close winded. But as the breeze strengthened so the boat came increasingly alive, Tino bouncing Tigger-like from bowsprit to boom end, a barefoot ragamuffin of competent enthusiasm, out he came with the biggest compliment of all:

'Oh, a passage maker.'

And of course we got back in. Carried our way.

Playing.

In sheltered waters.

30

A Cautionary Tale
(Madness at Sea)

No matter what the conditions, the most absurd mistakes can be made, and are made continually, and that by practiced men.

Hilaire Belloc. Again.

G (I will call him G out of discretion) and I were on passage back from Ireland. G was a fine seaman, very experienced, very strong, but you needed to be aware that he was a diabetic, and prone, now and again, to what they call a hypo. And to know what to do when it happened.

Which, in the middle of the night, somewhere off the south coast of Cornwall, bound east, with a nice land breeze, it did. G being strong and his hypos unnecessarily dramatic there ensued all kinds of excitement, during which *Sauntress*, naturally, was left to her own devices until he could be subdued and left to sleep it off.

And you return, all atremble, G having with difficulty been restrained from casting himself overboard, when not howling at the moon, to the business of steering your ship. Still that nice beam wind. Bring the lubber line back in line with the grid, for it is a grid steering compass and one of the best, and you lapse into a kind of trance, shore lights on your beam, a lighthouse winking somewhere, until the sky lightens, and the sun rises, for by now you are beyond tired.

In the west. Incredible. What has happened to the world?

And just for a second, such is the isolation at sea, such is your state of mind, you believe it. The words formed:

'G come and look, something has happened.'

But they were not spoken, for at last the realization came. We had been steering a reciprocal, back the way we came. Which is how we came to be flirting, becalmed and in the grip of the tide with the Seven Stones reef.

A touch of *The Shadow Line* in all this.

Of course I should have realised, land to starboard instead of to port, light seen but not identified, nor even did the thought occur, just the next headland as we sailed 'east,' same beam wind, same hypnotic, trance like state, waiting, an eternity, for dawn.

Plus ça change…

Bibliography

MacCarthy, Dermod: *Sailing with Mr Belloc*, Collins Harvill 1986

UK Hydrographic Office: *Bay of Biscay Pilot* 2010

Borrow, George: *The Bible in Spain* 1842

UKHO: *West Coast of Spain and Portugal Pilot* Sixth Edition 1992

Douglas, Norman: *Old Calabria,* M Secker. London 1915

The Monthly Magazine or British Register, Volume 11, 'State of Public Affairs in February', 1801

Steel, David: *The elements of rigging, seamanship and Naval tactics* 1794

Marshall's *Practical Marine Gunnery*, United States Navy 1822

Jarvis, Rupert C: 'Fractional Shareholding in British Merchant Ships' in *The Mariner's Mirror*, Volume 45 1959 Issue 4

Duplessis, Hugo: 'The perils of politics, Cruising Franco's Spain' in RCC *Roving Commissions*, 1949

Somerville and Ross: *Some experiences of an Irish RM*, 1858.

Frost, Michael: *Half a Gale*, Kenneth Mason 1981

Johns, Rev. C A: *British Birds in their Haunts*, F.L.S. London, 1867

Graham, Cdr R D: 'Emanuel in the Bay of Biscay', in RCC *Roving Commissions*, 1931

Faden, W: *España Marítima*, London 1812

Worth, Claud: *Yacht Cruising*, J D Potter, London 1934

Torre, Cdr Luis Jar: 'A Plantagenet in the Court of Ferrol', in *La Revista General de la Marina* (Spanish Naval Review)

Seymour, Rt. Hon. Sir Edward Hobart: *My Naval Career and Travels*, London, Elder Smith and Co. 1911